WALLACE-HOMESTEAD PRICE GUIDE TO AMERICAN COUNTRY ANTIQUES

By Don and Carol Raycraft

WALLACE-HOMESTEAD BOOK CO.
1912 GRAND AVENUE
DES MOINES, IOWA 50305

ISBN 0-87069-230-5
LIBRARY OF CONGRESS CATALOG
CARD 77-0726

Photography: Hayes & Benedict
Deposit, N.Y.

PUBLISHED BY

WALLACE-HOMESTEAD BOOK CO.
1912 GRAND AVENUE
DES MOINES, IOWA 50305

Contents

Acknowledgments

The authors wish to sincerely thank the following individuals for their kindness and assistance in putting this book together:

Jim and Ellie Cain, Cain's Antiques, Roscoe, NY
William and Lola McKnight, Bloomington, IL
Richard Axtell, Deposit, NY
Don Meyer, General's Fireside, Waterloo, NY
Esther Broadhurst Morehouse, Waterloo, NY
Wayne Fish, Fisherman's Cove, Branchport, NY
Robert Lyon, Des Moines, IA
Doris Benedict, Deposit, NY
Mrs. Donald J. Raycraft, Normal, IL
Don Brown, Leon, IA
Mrs. J. Maxwell Pickens, Watseka, IL
Captain Alex Hood, Los Gatos, CA
Lawrence and L.D. Hopkins, Bloomington, IL

Dedication

This project is a memorial to the $105 cupboards, $85 dry sinks, $45 birdjugs, $15 buttermolds and $5 baskets we failed to provide a home for in the 1960s. The loss is ours and their memory lives on.

1. Introduction

In recent years, a multitude of price guides have been produced for an audience seeking knowledge of the value of pieces in their collections or for a quick study and instant appraisal at an antiques show or auction. These guides typically have taken two forms. Either they encompass the realm of antiques from Victorian jewelry to painted cupboards and in the process attempt to do too much, or are issued every two years with all prices escalated 10 percent.

A price guide that utilizes the retail price of a basket in a shop in Bennington, Vermont or a cupboard in Hallowell, Maine does a disservice to the collector who has never been east of Omaha. The individual collector in Provo, Santa Fe, or Springdale, Arkansas is amazed and mystified at how cheap things are in the east when compared with the prices he pays for the odd basket, crock, or sugar basket that the local purveyor of antiques has hauled back from Vermont, New Hampshire, or Wurtsboro on a diet of golden arches and Holiday Inns.

We have tried to weigh the geographical impact in putting this project together for those collectors who view country antiques as an avocation, vocation, or obsession.

This project limits its scope to American country antiques. We have attempted, through selected auctions, questionnaires, advertisements and personal experience, to ascertain the approximate value of a wide variety of early furniture, pottery, baskets, Shaker, and kitchen and hearth antiques.

We have utilized prices from several important sales at Garth's Auction, Inc. of Delaware, Ohio, to provide additional insight into the current pricing of country antiques. Garth's has printed catalogues of the auctions available on a subscription basis. Garth's is located midway between the east and west coasts, and its sales are a prime indicator of price trends in the field of country antiques.

The authors' knowledge has been secured through 12 years of hearing dealers six hours away describe over the telephone the 50 pieces of decorated stoneware and unusual painted furniture in their shops, and arriving late in the evening to find three cracked crocks and an oak commode in original latex.

The tragedy is that every time we hear the story we throw three sons, a gross of Marvel Comics, and a tattered checkbook into the station wagon and set off to find that elusive rarity.

Unfortunately, we find just enough to make up for the countless times the trip is wasted, but the motivation persists and the hunt continues.

This is another step along that perpetual path.

2. Nostalgia

Before a collector can gain any insight into the price structure of the country antiques market, he or she should have a brief exposure to the way it used to be. Keep in mind during this short hiatus into the past that the two-wheeled coffee grinder offered in August, 1948, for $12.50 must be measured in 1948 dollars.

We have gone through auction catalogues and periodicals to find the 65 prices that appear below. They include items advertised for sale from June, 1928, through November, 1954.

It is interesting to note that advertisements during this period generally were devoid of many items that are especially popular today. These include decorated stoneware pottery, baskets, advertising, dry sinks and other pieces of country furniture.

It is equally interesting to speculate on the collectables and antiques not eagerly collected in the 1970's that will become the sought-after items of the 1980's and 1990's. At that point, we will look upon the prices being asked today as incredibly reasonable. Fifty years ago, today's prices were beyond the level of comprehension. The short escapade that follows will provide insights into that long ago and far away world when measured by the antiques market.

In April, 1926, a lady from Illinois wrote to an antiques shop in Ithaca, New York, inquiring about some colonial antiques that had been advertised. In addition to some pictures that will get some hearts across the nation pumping, the owner sent a small brochure describing his wares. Bits and pieces from the brochure appear below.

Beds

"We have a large collection of 4-post beds; many in curly maple with low, medium, and high posts, unusual turnings, Acanthus leaf and pineapple carving; mahogany 4-post, tapering posts some nearly 8' high.

Our collection of day beds includes many types. Many with spool turnings and others plain; several maple beds. All the beds have the original side rack and slots, and we paint the bed any color desired. Prices range from $5 to $15."

Chairs

"It is difficult to describe our collection of chairs inasmuch as we have over 1,000 now in stock of all styles and types. A large collection of fiddlebacks, singly and in sets of 2, 4 and 6 ranging in price from $8 to $15 each.

We have many chairs with the original lacquer and stencil, appropriate for dining room chairs in sets of 4, 6, 8 and 10 all in perfect condition with rush seats. Prices range from $30 per set."

Desks

"We have many other slant-top desks of all sizes in mahogany and cherry, as well as several school master's desks in cherry and walnut in original condition, prices from $15 to $25."

Plate 1.
The bench-table at the far left above was "of old paint and cleaned down to the natural wood, priced at $40. Interesting cut-out ends and a smaller one of the same wood type at $30."

Plate 3.
Child's Boston rocker, country Queen Anne table, and drop leaf table with duck feet ($30) and curly maple stand at right ($40).

This picture also contains some items that were considered of little value and would have been purchased for a few dollars in 1926. The spinning wheels, hay forks, and large field baskets were still available in large quantities and were in use in many parts of the country.

Plate 4.
Variety of tables and uncommon candle stand with adjustable height.

Plate 2.
Child's slat-back armchair, tables and hooked rugs that "begin at $2."

Now you know how Bing Crosby felt when he awoke in King Arthur's Camelot and saw William Bendix and his friends. How much would you pay for a round trip ticket back in time to that shop in Ithaca in the spring of 1926?

Sixty-Five Early Things
Advertised between 1928 and 1954

June 1928
1. American oval walnut hutch table - $25
2. Bench table in pine - $25
3. Pine corner cupboard - 5'10" high 28" across - refinished - $150

September 1928
4. American powder horns - $6 each
5. Iron candle snuffers - $3
6. Several good Windsors - $25 and $30
7. 1-drawer small maple candle stand - $25
8. Small maple and pine slope-top desk - very old - $165
9. Pine blanket chest - 1 long drawer - $40
10. 12-leg maple settee (deacon's bench) - $300
11. Sailor's old pine chest - refinished - old hammered strap - $50
12. Old hickory bench - splendid condition - 74" long x 19" deep - 10 legs - $100
13. Old American pewter candlesticks - $9 each
14. Cobbler's candlestand - small - perfect - original - $100
15. Pine corner cupboard - butterfly shelves - $27.50
16. Pineapple high-post bed - $275

October 1928
17. Curly maple - 4 drawer chest - ball feet - old brasses - $225
18. Pine tavern table - c. 1720 - $95
19. Maple slat-back arm chairs - 4 and 5 slats - $12 each
20. Queen Anne mirror - 42" x 23" - $1,000

November 1930
21. Curly maple picture frames - 18" x 15" - $20
22. Penna. comb-back Windsor armchair - $200
23. 8-leg pine table (refinished) - $75
24. Rare Windsor rocker - knuckle arms - original - $225
25. Desirable old lowboy of cherry wood - $150
26. Curly maple highboy - sunburst top and bottom - old brasses - $975
27. Maple frames (not less than 25) - $1.50 each
28. New England 9-room house - Revolutionary War Period - shipped anywhere in the U.S. - disassembled - $650

July 1931
29. Richard Lee 8" pewter plate - $35
30. Fine walnut tavern table - cushion feet - $85

June 1932
31. Flintlock Ky. rifle - curly maple stock - $20

32. Set of 6 eagle splatted stenciled Hitchcock side chairs - $360
33. 3 Windsor fan-back side chairs - $105

November 1933
34. A splendid little Franklin stove with andirons - $68

April 1934
35. Set of 6 decorated Hitchcock chairs - $100
36. Banjo clock with original painting and gilt bracket - $175

October 1934
37. Weathervanes: eagle, setter, cow, Pegasus, locomotive - $20-$50
38. Set of 6 Hitchcock chairs - $100 crated

June 1948
39. Wooden pitchforks - $4.50 to $6.50
40. Wooden grain scoops - $4.50 and $7.50
41. Conestoga wagon tar pot with lid - $12.50

August 1948
42. 2-wheel Enterprise coffee grinder - 24" tall - diameter of wheel 17" - eagle finish - original condition - $12.50
43. Set of 30 alphabet blocks - various prints - $8.50

January 1949
44. Signed Shaker rocker - arms - original taped seat - $32
45. Original stencil - 6 plank-bottom Pennsylvania Dutch chairs - $195

March 1949
46. Pair of Bennington Toby jugs - $25

April 1949
47. Large walnut corner cupboard, small paneled doors - spoon rack - $200

July 1949
48. Birdseye maple desk and chair - $55

December 1949
49. Curly maple table with bird cage - snake feet - 31¾" diameter - $165

April 1954
50. 18th century open pewter cup. - oak, walnut and pine - 7'3" high 5'6" deep - $1,100
51. Bennington Toby pitcher - $8.50

July 1954
52. 18th century tin sconce with mirror - $45
53. Long-handled PA. iron waffle iron - $10

54. 6 long-handled brass ladles - 2 with wrought iron handles - each $7
55. Cherry candlestand - 17" top - 28½" tall - $75

August 1954
56. 18" pewter charger "John Jupe" c.1750 - $32
57. Dentist occupational shaving mug, owner's name in gold, "John A. Mies" - $25

November 1954
58. 7 oval splat - ladder back chairs - $100
59. Scrimshaw whale's tooth - early sailing vessel with American flag - $7.50
60. Bennington ware pig bank - $8.50
61. Woven Penna. coverlet - red and white and blue - dated 1844 - $45
62. Set of 28 graduated sleigh bells - range from 1¼" to ¾" - $65
63. Powder flask - clasped hands and eagles - dated 1837 - $42.50
64. Blanket chest - pine - painted blue - $58
65. Hired man's bed - red paint - $35

After taking you back 50 years to study values, we thought a trip into the not-too-distant past would provide some appreciation of how prices have or have not changed in the past few years. Included in the list of auctioned items is another two-wheeled Enterprise coffee grinder. We have recently seen similar Enterprise coffee grinders in antique shops priced from $225 to $275.

One Hundred Pieces from 1975 Auctions at Garth's

1. Amber "coca cola" bottle - Erie, PA - $6
2. Tin cookie cutter - large rooster - $22.50
3. Tin cookie cutter - man with fat stomach - $15
4. Cast iron Aunt Jemima - $15
5. Wooden stocking stretchers - 38" long - $10
6. Cast iron bank - circus lion - old gold, red, and blue paint - 5½" high - $35
7. Copper candy kettle with iron handles and tripod stand - $75
8. Rare electric blue canning jar - 1 of 6 known - $650
9. Pine dovetailed ballot or ticket box - 11" x 8" x 8" - $45
10. Hanging pine knife scourer box - $25
11. Birdseye maple picture frame - 14½" x 16¾" - $85
12. Bluebill drake decoy - central Wis. c. 1925 - Yellow Lake - $75
13. Large copper candy kettle with iron handles - dovetailed 18½" diameter - $75
14. Wrought iron spatula - twisted handle - $115
15. Wrought iron and brass ladle and skimmer - signed F.B.S. Canton, O. - $150
16. Comb-back Windsor rocking chair - bamboo turnings - modern black paint - $165
17. Oval wooden bowl with handles - 20½" long - $45
18. Knuckle-arm Windsor bench - curly maple base - shaped pine seat - curly maple arm supports and crest rail - refinished - $1,200
19. 4 Hitchcock-type side chairs - black with worn gold stenciling - $120
20. Primitive pine dough box - dovetailed and splayed base - dark red over other colors - $55
21. Sewer tile frog - $12.50
22. Cracked butter mold - cased - sheaf of wheat - $12.50
23. Tin sander - $8
24. Tin cookie cutter of a woman - $5
25. Tin cookie cutter of a bear - $5
26. Tin cookie cutter of a chicken - $13
27. Tin betty lamp and stand - $125
28. Two-section knife box with hinged lids - yellow combed decoration - 20th century - $12.50
29. Tin nutmeg grater - $6
30. Single cast pewter candle mold - $18
31. Oval wooden bowl - refinished - 25½" diameter - $30
32. Wooden sugar bucket with wire handle - $25
33. Burl mallet - $10
34. Hand wrought double-edge ax with handle 14" long - $20
35. Poplar jelly cupboard - one board doors - hinges replaced - old red paint - 45" x 15" x 47" high - $170
36. Small rye basket - 6½" diameter - $7.50
37. Blue calico print star cut from quilt - new painted frame - $25
38. Treen sand shaker - 7¼" high - $15
39. Butter print - stylized tulips - 3½" x 4¾" - $75
40. Wrought iron rush light holder in wooden base - 13" high - $65
41. Punched tin foot warmer - wooden frame with turned posts - $45
42. Cherry one-drawer nite stand - tapering legs - replaced top - $85
43. Brass sander - $5
44. Stoneware jug - stenciled ad for druggist - "Wheeling, W. Va." - $25
45. Iron double crusie lamp - twisted hanger - $15
46. Earthenware flower pot - 9½" high - $20
47. Noah's Ark - approx. 40 hand carved animals - $120
48. Pair of wooden bellows with long flared brass nozzle - good leather - 34" long - $27.50
49. A part of an early tombstone dated 1837 - $30
50. Oval butter bowl - 23" long - $30
51. Cast iron coffee grinder - Enterprise - No. 5 - 17" high - worn original paint - $190
52. Cast iron matchbox - "Pat. 1872" - $20
53. Wooden nut cracker - jaws of man in tri-corner hat cracks the nut - $7.50
54. Wooden Conestoga wagon tar bucket - $17.50
55. Wooden apple peeler - $40
56. Tin "ABC" plate is "Who killed Cock Robin" - $17.50
57. Primitive hearth broom - 43" long - $20
58. Wooden baker's peel - 69" long - $25
59. 3 gilded wooden letters "C.A.T." - 18" high - $55
60. 2 wooden kitchen mashers - $6
61. Small poplar blanket chest - till - grained decoration - 38" long x 19" wide x 21" high - $105
62. PA. redware plate - wavey lines - old chips - 12½" diameter - $105
63. Stoneware jar - stenciled "Greensboro PA." - $19
64. Shaker wooden boot jack - $30
65. Wooden lemon squeezer - $28
66. Wooden 3-pronged hay fork - $45
67. Wooden shovel - 39" long - $45
68. Wooden butter paddle - $8
69. Small copper funnel - battered end - $5
70. Tole apple tray - stenciled flowers - worn 11¾" diameter - $40
71. Set of 3 arrow-back side chairs - $67.50
72. Wooden cookie board - both sides have animal shapes - $70
73. Cast iron hitching post - 65" high - $75
74. Blacksmith carry-all box - crude - $17.50

75. Skater's lantern - $17.50
76. Banjo dated - "Pat. Jan. 4, '87" - $12.50
77. Yellow ware mixing bowl - blue stripe - 9¼" d. - $5
78. Signed iron broad axe - $22.50
79. Pine captain's chair - simple country turnings - refinished - $30
80. 4-tube tin candlemold - $20
81. Stoneware bottle - 9¼" high - $3
82. American flag - 45 stars - 1896 - 86" x 140" - $15
83. Pine dry sink - refinished - paneled doors - 56" long x 20" wide x 45" high - $220
84. 8-tube candle mold in tin - $20
85. Stoneware butter crock - embossed fruit and "Butter" - 7" diameter - $27.50
86. Copper wash boiler - polished - 27" long - $30
87. Brass bed warmer with an incised floral design and turned handle - 43½" long - $170
88. Wrought iron spatula - small size - 10¾" long - $20
89. Brass dipper with wrought iron handle - 18" long - $80
90. Early pine sawbuck table - 2 board top - 37" x 92" x 28½" - $750
91. Brass cigar cutter - polished - 18th century - $27.50
92. Tin 12-tube candle mold - $33
93. Tole bread box - green with black and yellow striping - clasp incomplete - $5
94. Early Colorado gold mine claim deed signed Richard Kellogg, Samson, Colo. - $12
95. Country hanging cupboard - one drawer and paneled door with applied heart - old blue-green paint - $150
96. Unusual granite ware preserving jar - 4¼" - $20
97. Iron safe with painted scene - key lock - on wheels - 10" high - $40
98. Stoneware bottle - "Fat Boy Monti's Sarsaparilla Beer" - 10" high - $20
99. Turned wooden pin cushion - clamps to table top - $40
100. Large stoneware water jug - reddish brown glaze - 36" high - 2 handles - $70

3. Country Furniture

A casual survey of issues of *Antiques Magazine* from the 1920's through the mid-1950's shows little attention paid to country furniture. There is a wealth of information on costly pieces produced by urban cabinet makers, but little dealing with the products of the rural joiner.

Most collectors interested in country furniture in the 1940's and 1950's felt that it was necessary to strip the original milk base paint from the desk or cupboard to bring out the warm beauty of the pine or poplar underneath. However, the late 1960's and the decade of the 1970's ushered in a new appreciation of furniture in its original or early finish among a large number of collectors. The cult of eastern collectors who had been turned on to painted furniture for many years now faced competition from individuals who had previously been on a first-name basis at the local store that sold paint remover.

If two similar pieces of furniture were sold at auction and one was in its original state and the other refinished, the painted piece would generally sell for a minimum of 50-60% more.

A cupboard decorated for the last time with a covering of grey paint in the 1930's should be carefully stripped coat by coat until an appealing homemade color hidden under years of factory-produced paint makes its slow appearance.

Country furniture produced from soft woods from the mid-1700's until the mid-1800's was painted shortly after its construction. Hardwood pieces of walnut or cherry were often left natural because of the wood's beautiful grain.

Collectors rarely will have an opportunity to purchase an oak piece that dates prior to the 1870's. Furniture of the Pilgrim century, as documented by Wallace Nutting and others, that was constructed in the 1600's and early 1700's has all but vanished.

Oak found in shops and at shows is a product of an industrial revolution that followed the Civil War. In the late 1860's, industrialists found themselves with a rail network and factories that had produced canteens and bullets for a market that went out of existence when Grant met Lee at Appomattox.

The northern factories turned to producing bedroom suites and parlor sets for the catalogue stores that came into operation to take advantage of the railroad tracks that linked rural villages with Chicago, Baltimore and St. Louis.

The pine furniture that had been carefully crafted from New Hampshire to Ohio or Illinois no longer was fashionable. It provided only utility and reeked of its simple beginnings. Factory-made oak and walnut furniture quickly replaced the earlier furnishings.

This project is concerned primarily with country furniture constructed through the American Civil War. The majority of the pieces illustrated and described are pine. We have tried to include pieces and examples finished in early paint.

The value of a piece of country furniture is determined primarily by the degree to which it has been "played with." If the bottom of a cupboard has dry rotted and been cut down or the early finish has been stripped to a plastic glow, the value of the piece diminishes proportionately.

Significant differences in taste in the various sections of the country dramatically influence the value of a piece of furniture. As one creeps slowly west of Ohio, the appreciation of and demand for painted furniture diminishes and the popularity of refinished country pine and later factory-made oak increases. Thus, what might be rare and costly in Maine or New Hampshire could go unrecognized in Iowa or Nebraska.

A short quiz based on a single picture

follows each of the following sections. After you have digested all six sections, studied the prices and taken the quizzes, hopefully you will have a successful experience with the final examination presented at the end of the book.

Plate 6.

Bucket bench
Pine, early red paint, 24" high 44" long, found in Ohio, c. 1860-1870.
Value: $330-$360.

Another uncommon form for a bucket bench. It appears to be a dry sink, because of its design and zinc-lined trough. The two shelves below held soap, rags and brushes. Pine was typically used in constructing water or bucket benches. This example retains much of its early milk base paint.

Plate 5.

Bucket bench, wood box
Pine, early red paint, found in Ohio, c. 1880.
Value: $275-$300

This example is unusual because it has a wood box. Bucket benches were used for storing wash day supplies and were generally kept on the back porch. The round nails date it from the late 19th century. Pieces of this type should be examined carefully, because the heavy use they were put to often makes them appear earlier than they actually are.

Plate 7.

Bucket bench
Pine, early red paint, uncommon form, found in Pennsylvania, c. 1840.
Value: $450-$550.

This bucket bench originally had a bar across the front of the top shelf. Like many pieces of early furniture, it had several generations of paint on it when purchased. The coat that preceded the red was oak graining applied with one of the tin combs that were used in the late 1800's.

13

Plate 8.

Bucket bench
Pine, 30" high, unpainted, Ohio, c. 1880-1900.
Value: $85-$100.

This small bench has boot jack ends and cross stretcher supports. It is held together by screws, rather than the round headed nails one would suspect.

Plate 9.

Bucket bench
Pine, in old grey paint, possibly Shaker, c. 1850-1860.
Value: $550-$650.

This piece is an uncommon form for a bucket bench. It contains a single drawer and a storage compartment with double doors.

Plate 10.

Bucket bench
Pine, mortised construction, early green paint, Pennsylvania, c. 1830-1840.
Value: $210-$225.

This bench measures 36" long x 29" high and was used on a table or dry sink.

Plate 11.

Dry sink
Pine, unusual extended trough for a pump, Ohio, c. 1860.
Value: $550-$600.

6-drawer Shaker spice chest
Old red stain, turned knobs, c. 1870-1880.
Value: $225-$300.

This early dry sink in red paint was found in Ohio and dates from the mid-1800's. Collectors find more dry sinks in Ohio, Indiana and Illinois than any other section of the country. They date from 1850 until well into the 20th century. Most sinks are of poplar or pine, with late examples of oak turning up occasionally at flea markets or closing-out farm sales.

Plate 12.

Dry sink
Pine, single drawer, c. 1870.
Value: $300-$330.

The pine sink was purchased in eastern Indiana. It has a single drawer for soap or kitchen utensils. The drawer pull is a late replacement, and the work area above has been repaired.

Plate 13.

Dry sink
Pine, in old green paint, c. 1870-1880, found in Ohio.
Value: $350-$450.

This is a conventional midwestern sink in design. It was probably painted for the last time 50-75 years ago. The zink lining has been removed and rockingham pulls added at some point. This example was found in Ohio and dates from the late 1800's.

Plate 14.

Dry sink
Pine, green and red paint, Illinois, c. 1870.
Value: $500-$600.

Another midwestern form of the dry sink that dates from the mid-1800's. This type of sink commands a higher price than the more commonly found form in Plate 13. The high back splash with a shelf adds 20% to 25% to the price. A high back sink with 3-4 drawers along the top is worth at least $150-$200 more than the standard sink in Plate 13.

Plate 15.

Bedside table
Pine, refinished, New England, c. 1870.
Value: $250-$275.

Tables of this type were used in bedrooms for holding pitcher and bowl sets. This example was originally covered with green paint, but was refinished about 20 years ago. The value would increase by $200-$250 if the table had its original paint.

Plate 17.

Miniature chest
Pine, early green paint, Pennsylvania, c. 1860-1870.
Value: $140-$160.

This is a close-up of the chest at the top of the stack in Plate 16. It measures 5″ high x 5½″ deep x 9½″ long.

Plate 16.
Linen press or storage cupboard
Pine, early red paint, Pennsylvania, c. 1840-1850.
Value: $400-$450.

A linen press is a storage piece for blankets and household linens. Cracks similar to the one in the door generally have little significance to the value of early country furniture.

Miniature chests
Pine, early green and blue paint, Pennsylvania, c. 1860-1870.
Value: $140-$160.

Shaker sewing basket
Oak splint, New England, c. 19th century.
Value: $100-$115.

Plate 18.
Immigrant's chest or blanket chest
Pine, early red paint, Pennsylvania, c. 1840, dimensions: 48″ long x 28″ high x 24″ deep.
Value: $350-425.

Many times a piece of furniture of uncommon size has its value limited by the difficulty it creates in trying to use it in a conventional home.

Plate 19.

Chopping table
Pine, original finish, Illinois, c. 1880-1900, dimensions: 35½" wide x 28" high x 65½" long.
Value: $375-$400.

Burl bowl
American, found in New England, c. 1830-1850, dimensions: 14" diameter x 5½" high.
Value: $425-$600.

Burl is a wart-like growth found on maple and walnut trees that provided an unusually hard wood for craftsmen to shape bowls. In recent years, there has been a great influx of European burl bowls and root bowls that have been sold inexpensively across the country. Before investing in burl, it is wise to have a knowledgeable collector authenticate the American heritage of the piece.

Plate 20.

Comb-decorated blanket chest
Pine, early red and mustard paint, Ohio, c. 1860.
Value: $375-$450.
(Hilliard Collection, Provo, Utah)

17

Plate 21.
Decorated blanket chest
Pine, mustard and orange paint, Ohio, c. 1860,
dimensions: 48″ long x 19″ x 28″ high.
Value: $350-$500.

Plate 22.
Blanket chest
Pine, refinished, New York state, c. 1870-1875.
Value: $225-$250.

Plate 23.
Blanket chest
Pine, early blue paint, Pennsylvania, c. 1850.
Value: $450-$650.

Plate 24.
Jelly or preserve cupboard
Pine, refinished, Ohio.
Value: $150-$175.

This small (35″ high) and crudely constructed storage cupboard was found in
northeastern Ohio. It contains two shelves
and carries traces of its original red paint.

Plate 25.
Chair table
Pine, red base and scrubbed top, New England,
c. 1830.
Value: $750-$850.

An early work or dining table described
as "in original condition" should not have
an unblemished coat of paint on its top.
In fact, it should have very little paint.
The tops were scrubbed after every meal
and eventually the paint was worn away.

18

Plate 27.

Schoolmaster's desk
Pine, early red paint, Pennsylvania, c. 1830-1840.
Value: $400-$600.

Plate 26.

Step-back cupboard
Pine, early red paint, two-piece construction, Ohio, c. 1840.
Value: $600-$750.

Plate 28.

Bedside table
Pine, early paint, Ohio, c. 1870-1880.
Value: $200-$250.
(Hilliard Collection, Provo, Utah)

Stoneware jar
Lyons, New York, c. 1865-1870.
Value: $125-$135.

The value of this piece is increased by the turned legs, early paint and additional work on the drawer front. The knob is a late replacement.

Redware cottage cheese mold
Unmarked, probably Pennsylvania, c. 1850.
Value: $75-$80.

Plate 29.

Small bench
Pine, worn green paint, Pennsylvania, c. 1860-1880.
Value: $250-$280.

Plate 30.

Step-back cupboard
Pine and wild cherry, 16 "lights," Ohio, c. 1840-1850.
Value: $1,000-$1,500.

This two-piece cupboard originally was covered with two coats of deep brown paint. The "lights" or panes of glass appear to be original. The cupboard in Plate 26 may be described as a "blind front", because it has solid doors rather than panes of glass.

Wooden churn
Maple and pine with iron bands, c. 1840-1850.
Value: $180-$210.

Stoneware butter crock
Unsigned, bird decoration, c. 1840.
Value: $150-$180.

Stoneware crocks with an original lid are rarely found.

Whites' Utica 3-gal. crock
c. 1850.
Value: $115-$130.

Unsigned 4-gal. crock with tulip decoration
Value: $85-$125.

Plate 31.

Wagon seat
Pine and maple, refinished, splint seat, New England, c. 1830-1840.
Value: $425-$450 - in early paint, $550-$600.

Chairs of this type were used in horse-drawn passenger and farm wagons in the early 1800's. They provided a place to sit on the way to town or church, and could be removed and carried inside after arrival.

Plate 32.

Deacon's bench or settle
Maple and pine, refinished, length 72″, c. 1870.
Value: $300-$400.

Similar benches in a variety of lengths ranging from 4′ to 14′ were manufactured and sold to churches, town halls and shopkeepers for use in front of their emporiums from the 1850's through 1900.

Plate 34.

Jam or jelly cupboard
Pine, early blue paint, New York state, c. 1840-1850.
Value: $385-$425.

The most desirable color of early furniture for most collectors is blue. Blue paint on a bucket or piece of furniture usually adds 10% to 20% to the value.

This cupboard is an unusual form with a display or work surface on top and two large storage areas below.

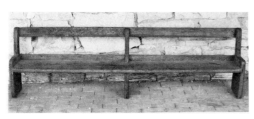

Plate 33.

Recitation bench
Pine, original unpainted finish, from an Amish school in Ohio, c. 1850.
Value: $350-$550.

This bench is 5½′ long and the plank seat is 13″ off the ground. It was used as a bench for primary-age children to recite their lessons in front of a class filled with their bored peers.

Chopping block

Plate 35.

Maple, refinished, turned round legs, c. 1880-1900.
Value: $250-$275.
(Spilman-Cutler collection Knoxville, Ill.)

21

Work table
Plate 36.

Early blue-grey paint, maple and pine, scrubbed top, found in Ohio, c. 1850.
Value: $175-$200.

This country work table has a two-board top, pegged sides and turned legs. Use of pine and maple in a piece of furniture is not unusual. Often, several woods were used because the table or chair was painted soon after its construction.

Plate 37.

Chest of drawers

Oak graining over pine, New England, c. 1860.
Value: $300-$325.

When oak regained its popularity in the late 1800's, there was a rush to simulate oak grain on many pieces that had been purchased a generation or two earlier. Many examples from the early 1800's were given a stylish paint job in the 1880's.

Plate 38.

Chopping block

Walnut on maple legs, 9″ thick, Indiana, c. 1860 (?).
Value: $65-$75.

A small block is almost impossible to date accurately, because construction techniques changed little for a period of more than 250 years. It could be as early as the 1700's, or as late as the early 1900's.

Blocks of this type were used for separating chickens from their heads.

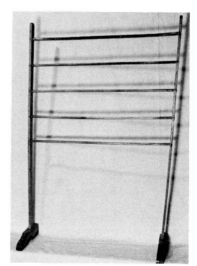

Plate 39.

Towel rack

Maple, shoe feet, found in Ohio, c. 1900.
Value: $40-$50.

Quilt or coverlet rack
Maple, factory-made, c. 1880-1900.
Value: $50-$60.

Plate 40.

Plate 41.
Country store coffee bin
Pine, red paint, stenciled label, replaced bottom
board, c. 1900.
Value: $75-$85.

Plate 42.
Staved storage barrel
Pine, early blue paint, iron bands, 28″ high, c. 1870.
Value: $225-$250.

Plate 43.
Small immigrant's truck
Pine, worn top, early green bottom, Scandinavian,
c. 1840-1850.
Value: $160-$175.

This trunk measures 30″ long x 8″ high
x 14″ deep. It was brought to the United
States in the mid-1800's by a Swedish immigrant and found in Wisconsin.

Plate 44.

Slat-back kitchen chair
Maple and pine, splint seat, blue-grey paint, c. 1840.
Value: $100-$115.
    set of four in similar condition, $650.

Plate 46.

Slat-back side chair
Maple, splint seat, refinished, New York state, c. 1850.
Value: $55-$60.
    set of four in similar condition, $300.

Plate 45.

Bannister-back side chair
Tiger maple, sausage-turned legs, replaced rush seat, New York state, c. 1830.
Value: $225-$250.

Plate 47.

Slat-back side chair
Pine, chestnut, and maple, replaced splint seat, Ohio, c. 1860.
Value: $50-$75.

24

Plate 49.

Arrow-back settee
Black paint, pine and maple, New York state, c. 1830.
Value: $450-$500.

Plate 48.

Stenciled side chairs
Mixture of woods, pine plank seat, Pennsylvania, c. 1850-1860.
Value: $60 each.
        set of four in mint original paint, $350.

These chairs were originally sold in sets of 6-12. Sets of chairs in good condition with the early decoration intact are hard to find. These examples have reached the point where they will have to be stripped or repainted. If repainting is the process chosen, before and after pictures should be taken to document their age and the original decoration.

Plate 50.

Hoop-back Windsor arm chair
Maple and pine, simply turned legs, probably English.
Value: $175-$200.

Plate 53.
Loop-back Windsor side chair
American, maple with pine plank seat, refinished,
c. 1830.
Value: $110-$120.
     set of four refinished chairs, $500-$525.
     set of four chairs in old paint, $650-$750.

Plate 51.
Boston fiddle-back rocking chair
Early red and black decoration, stenciling, freehand
flowers, found in Illinois, c. 1860-1875.
Value: $225-$250.

Plate 54.
Slat-back arm chair
Replaced splint seat, refinished, New York state,
early turnings, c. 1820-1830.
Value: $160-$175.

Plate 52.
Slat-back child's arm chair
Splint seat, early stenciling and black paint, c. 1860.
Value: $75-$85.

Plate 55.
Slat-back kitchen chair
Pine and maple, refinished, "Rabbit ears", c. 1880.
Value: $50-$60.
    set of four refinished, $280-$310.

Plate 57.
Rod-back kitchen chair
Maple, pine plank seat, midwestern, c. 1850-1860.
Value: $60-$75

Simply constructed side chairs are often described and sold as Shaker. Merely because a chair has no "superfluous" decoration does not make it Shaker. Collectors should consult Meader's *Illustrated Guide to Shaker Furniture* for an authoritative background on the Shaker arts.

Plate 56.
Corner cupboard
Pine, refinished, Maine, dimensions: 73" high x 33" wide.
Value: $700-$785
    In original paint, $900-$1,100.

Plate 58.
Rod-back Windsor high chair
Maple with pine plank seat, late paint, New England, C. 1840.
Value: $150-$175.
    In early paint, $225-$250.

Plate 59.
Child's Windsor hoop-back arm chair from England
Maple, 2″ pine plank seat, H stretcher, c. 1800-1820.
Value: $200-$225.

Plate 61.
Milking stool
18″ high, difficult to date, found in Pennsylvania.
Value: $40-$45.

Compare this English Windsor to the American Windsors in Plates 53 and 58. Note the splay or angle of the legs on the American chairs. The legs of the English Windsors have a much tighter angle to floor than American chairs.

It is interesting to note the difference between a hoop-back and loop-back chair. Hoop-back Windsors have a bar across the center of the spindles.

American Windsor chairs are considerably rarer and more costly than their English counterparts.

Low-post beds have carved headboards and footboards with turned posts. All four posts are about the same height. Most low-post beds are constructed of combinations of pine, cherry, chestnut, maple and birch.

Plate 60.
Printer's Stool
Maple, 42″ high, factory produced, never painted, c. 1890-1900.
Value: $45-$55.

Plate 62.
Low-post cannonball bed
Maple, walnut, pine, remnants of red paint, rope type construction to hold mattress, Ohio, c. 1840-1860.
Value: $250-$275.

Plate 63.
Low-post cannonball bed
Maple and pine, New York state, c. 1870-1875.
Value: $275-$325.

Plate 65.
Dough box
Pine, Ohio, refinished, joined with square nails, c. 1850-1860.
Value: $225-$275.

Plate 64.
Table-top chopping board
Maple, one-board top 36" in diameter, c. 1860.
Value: $100-$115.

Plate 66.
Document box
Pine, sponge-decorated yellow and brown paint, New Hampshire, c. 1830-1840.
Value: $175-$200.

Plate 67.

Storage cupboard
Pine, refinished, found in New York state, c. 1840.
Value: $220-$240

A married piece of furniture consists of two pieces of separate origin fitted together to form a single cupboard, desk or table. It is also possible to find a two-piece cupboard similar to the example in Plate 26 and split it into two distinct pieces of early furniture.

The top becomes an early hanging cupboard and the bottom a unique storage cupboard, and the price for both increases dramatically. Plate 67 appears to have been created in such a fashion.

Plate 69.

Tilt-top or tip-top table
Cherry, turned shaft, tripod legs, New England, c. 1800-1820.
Value:

Plate 68.

Candlestand
Tripod form, maple, New England, cleated two-board top, c. 1800.
Value: $350-$375.

Plate 70.

Small food storage chest
Dimensions: 15" long x 12" deep x 13 high, old blue exterior, worn red interior, staved construction early iron bands, found in Wisconsin, probably Scandinavian, c. 1800.
Value: $250-$275.

Plate 72.

Sawbuck table
Dimensions: 28½" high x 20" deep x 32½" long, pegged-top construction, pine, original finish, maple supports, c. 1820.
Value: $350-$375.

Plate 71.

Work table
Pine, scrubbed top, unusual carved gallery, single drawer, found in Pennsylvania, red base, c. 1840-1860.
Value: $250-$275.

Plate 73.

Cradle
Pine, open end, mustard exterior paint, uncommon finials and carved side decoration, New England, c. 1830-1840.
Value: $350-$400.

Plate 74.

Early Victorian chest of drawers
Tiger maple, made in an early factory, c. 1840.
Value: $350-$375.

Plate 75.

Horseshoer's box
Pine, wrought iron handle, early red paint, two
boxes for nails, c. 1870-1890.
Value: $65-$75.

Preliminary Quiz I

1. What type of arm chair is this?
   a. bannister back
   b. hoop-back
   c. brace-back
   d. none of the above

2. The seat of this chair is made of:
   a. splint
   b. rush
   c. rattan
   d. cane

3. This chair dates from approximately:
   a. 1730-1750
   b. 1830-1850
   c. 1880-1900

Answers may be found on page 164.

Prices of 67 Pieces of Furniture Advertised in 1977

1. Dovetailed violin case - $32 - Maine dealer
2. Early six-board blanket chest, bracket feet, old grey - $215 - Maine dealer
3. New England child's rocking chair, original paint, brass handle - $105 - Maine dealer
4. Excellent Pa. decorated child's slat-back chair, 28" high - $300 - Maine dealer
5. Grain bin in old red, ball feet - $150 - Mass. dealer
6. Dry sink, pine, 35½" long x 26½" high x 20" deep - $300 - Mass. dealer
7. Early pine settee, 44" wide x 46½" high x 13½" deep, shoe feet - $425 - Mass. dealer
8. 19th century leather covered trunk (Penna.) early hardware - $225 - Pa. dealer
9. Pine dry sink, 28" wide x 36" high - $295 - Iowa dealer
10. Poplar and maple settee, repaired arm, 72" long x 19½" deep - $345 - Ohio dealer
11. Pair of early N.E. loop-back Windsors, excellent condition - $525 - Ohio dealer
12. Maple-trestle butterfly table, N.E. 1680-1700, orig. paint - $1,500 - Maine auction
13. 18th century child's chair table - $1,750 - New Hampshire dealer
14. Penna. pie safe, tapered legs, maple, 59" x 30" x 21" - $400 - N.Y. dealer
15. Penna. yellow and brown grain painted cupboard, 48" wide x 59" tall x 15" deep - $325 - Maine dealer
16. Pair of bamboo Windsors, refinished, shaped seats - $200 pair - Mass. auction
17. Country single bed, old reddish brown mahogany finish, 38" x 74" - $250 - Pa. dealer
18. Trundle bed in orig. red paint, 42" x 66" - $165 - Pa. dealer
19. Bow-back Windsor arm chair, 6 spindles, full height, late paint - $750 - New York dealer
20. Maine chimney cupboard, orig. red paint, 83½" high x 36¼" wide - $650 - Ohio dealer
21. Hooded cradle, orig. red with blue interior - $500 - Ohio dealer
22. Pine cottage chest, oak graining, Maine - $175 - New Hampshire dealer
23. Ship carpenter's chest, old blue, molded base, 20½" tall - $175 - New Hampshire dealer
24. 2-drawer blanket chest, old blue, bootjack ends - $265 - New Hampshire dealer
25. Dowery chest, ogee bracket base, 26" high x 22" deep - $425 - New York dealer
26. Set of four thumb-back chairs - $225 - New York dealer
27. New England maple and ash corner chair - $350 - Mass. dealer
28. 1-drawer stand in old green paint, yellow detail - $135 - Mass. dealer
29. Round (42" diameter) hutch table in old red - $875 - Mass. dealer
30. Scalloped-base painted blanket box, Penna., 42" x 17" x 23" - $245 - Maine dealer
31. Red and black grained blanket box, 37" x 16" x 22" - $235 - Maine dealer
32. Country Windsor rocker, comb back - $475 - Maine dealer
33. Child's Hitchcock chair with orig. stenciling and rush seat - $175 - Ohio dealer
34. Miniature open cupboard in old paint, 23" high - $245 - Ontario, Canada, show
35. Early dome-top box, original blue paint, dated 1709 - $450 - Ontario, Canada, show
36. Signed Wallace Nutting comb-back Windsor arm chair, orig. paint - $650 - Maine auction
37. Natural finish, sausage-turned ladder-back arm chair - $325 - Maine auction
38. Pair of Rhode Island brace-back Windsor side chairs, traces of paint - $950 - Pa. dealer
39. Amish dry sink, poplar, dovetailed base - $400 - Ohio dealer
40. Dome-top box, c. 1840, putty graining, 28" x 13" x 13" - $95 - N.Y. dealer
41. Baby chair, arrow-back Windsor with arms and mustard paint - $80 - N.Y. dealer
42. Set of four thumb-back chairs with orig. decoration - $380 - New Hampshire dealer
43. Michigan pine dry sink with country Gothic doors - $250 - Michigan dealer
44. Penna. child's chair in brown paint with yellow decoration - $45 - Michigan dealer
45. Lancaster County, Pa. dry sink, 66" long, orange over yellow - $2,175 - Ohio dealer
46. Cherry bedside stand, hinged lift lid - $265 - Rhode Island dealer
47. Homemade pine dovetailed bathtub, copper lined - $225 - Missouri dealer
48. Trundle bed, slat-type, simple turnings, old red finish - $95 - Ohio dealer
49. 3-compartment grain bin, 3 slant lids, 6 drawers above, red - $650 - Ohio dealer
50. Walnut one-piece corner cupboard, 6'10" high, 4 doors - $595 - Ohio dealer
51. Splayed sea chest in green paint - $60 - Maine auction
52. Stand-up cobbler's bench, 3 drawers, old blue paint - $400 - Maine dealer
53. Diamond Dye cabinet, mint - $250 - Maine show
54. 4'6" swing-leg table with 18" leaves in birch - $400 - Maine dealer

55. Baby's sled, 30" long, "Bessie G. Dunning 1878", worn - $75 - Maine dealer
56. Wash basin stand, pine, painted like tiger maple, 38½" high - $225 - Pa. dealer
57. 5' wooden sled, iron runners, trace of red paint - $20 - Maine dealer
58. 3-shelf pine chimney cupboard, hand wrought nails - $130 - New Hampshire dealer
59. Sawbuck work table, scrubbed top, red base, 59" x 23" - $475 - Illinois dealer
60. Poplar jelly cupboard, 2-drawer, brown over light olive green - $795 - W. Virginia dealer
61. Walnut harvest table, 8' long, 2-board top, 1 large drawer - $195 - Michigan dealer
62. Pine pewter cupboard, orig. blue paint under enamel - $275 - Michigan dealer
63. High-back dry sink, butternut and poplar, 1 drawer and top shelf - $550 - Michigan dealer
64. Pine step-back cupboard, 2 plank doors, over 6 drawers, ready to refinish - $395 - Michigan dealer
65. Child's arrow-back chair, painted and stenciled - $115 - New Hampshire dealer
66. 40" carved cigar store Indian - $2,200 - Mass. auction
67. Tea table, maple, oval top, 34½" x 25½" x 26¼", c. 1780, Rhode Island - $6,200 - Illinois department store

50 Pieces of Furniture Sold at Garth's in 1977 with Prices

1. Set of pine hanging shelves, old dark graining, 3 shelves - $230
2. Windsor arm chair, turned legs and arm supports, converted to potty chair, seat has been plugged, old finish - $375
3. Primitive bucket bench, boot jack ends, worn green paint - $90
4. Bow-back Windsor arm chair, turned legs, worn black paint - $700
5. Single-size cherry cannonball bed, original rope pulls, well-developed turnings and scrolled headboard - $475
6. Spindle-back settle bench, scrolled arms, modern black paint with gold striping - $235
7. Walnut schoolmaster's desk, "H" stretcher, slant top - $210
8. Primitive pine bench, boot jack ends, blue grey paint - $105
9. Small pine cupboard, dovetailed case, 4 raised panels in door, 3 shelves, - $130
10. Primitive hanging cherry cupboard, refinished, 18" w. x 13" d. x 35½" h. - $100
11. Ladder-back arm chair, refinished, woven split seat - $75
12. Arrow-back arm chair, turned legs, added rockers, refinished - $65
13. Country candlestand, cherry spider legs, 2-board top, traces of red paint - $270
14. Set of 6 plank-seat side chairs, original stenciled decoration - $660
15. One-drawer pine stand, square tapering legs, original black paint - $250
16. Small dovetailed blanket chest, turned feet and till, poplar and walnut, grained decoration - $110
17. Child's continuous-arm Windsor chair, worn original dark brown paint - $750
18. Ladder-back arm chair, sausage turnings, 4 slats, worn black paint, new cane seat - $400
19. Decorated rocker, turned legs and arm supports, scrolled seat and arms, brownish red ground with stencil decoration - $130
20. Plank-seat side chair, bamboo turnings, worn original paint, brown base, yellow striping and primitive tulip - $115
21. Set of 6 balloon-back side chairs, orig. stencil decoration - $630
22. Country bedside table, sq. tapering legs, dovetailed drawer, 1-board top, birch, orig. red paint - $400
23. Windsor settle bench, bamboo turnings, arrow spindles, holes for baby guard, refinished - $400
24. Set of 6 Windsor side chairs, plank seats, spindle backs, refinished - $840
25. Grained blanket chest, pine, turned feet, dovetailed case, till, wrought iron hinges - $750
26. Small walnut table, turned legs, 1 drawer and 1-board top, refinished, 19" x 27" x 29" h. - $90
27. Child's arrow-back rocker, tan graining on a white ground, worn - $65
28. Child's decorated captain's chair, rocker, orig. paint, fruit stenciling on crest - $105
29. Primitive 1-piece walnut cupboard, board and bottom doors, refinished, late 19th century, 27" w. x 16½" d. x 77" h. - $400
30. Pair of arrow-back side chairs, refinished - $110
31. Round-top hutch table, turned legs, mortised stretcher base, 3-board pine top, traces of old paint - $675
32. Set of 6 decorated spindle-back side chairs, orig. paint, stenciled decoration - $450
33. Captain's chair, turned legs and spindles, bent wood arms - $35
34. Wooden coffee bin, stenciled decoration, worn red paint - $155
35. Bannister-back side chair, simple turnings, worn black paint, new seat, built-up front feet - $75

35. Cherry pie safe, turned legs, 8 punched tin panels in pinwheel design, refinished - $410

37. Arrow-back rocking chair, plank seat, refinished - $135

38. Curly maple bedside stand, turned legs, 1 dovetailed drawer, 1-board top - $245

39. Cherry stand, turned legs, 2 dovetailed drawers, 1-board top is an old replacement - $120

40. Late apothecary chest, 35 drawers, poplar drawer fronts, cherry, refinished, new top and bottom - $325

41. Arrow-back arm chair, bamboo base, refinished - $95

42. Poplar chest of 45 drawers, refinished and minor repairs, white porcelain knobs - $375

43. Country captain's chair, refinished and back has repair - $55

44. Small arrow-back settle bench, turned legs and scrolled arms, modern reddish brown paint - $260

45. Pine work table, sq. chamferred legs, "H" stretcher, 1 nailed drawer, 2-board top - $150

46. Ladder-back rocking chair, wide arms, woven cane seat, orig. dark red paint with yellow striping, late - $55

47. Refinished Boston rocker - $110

48. Decorated rabbit ear Windsor side chair, bamboo turnings, orig. brown paint, yellow striping and leaves - $85

49. Early pine blanket chest, shoe feet, single wide dovetailed joints, rose head nails, old red paint - $95

50. Child's decorated sleigh, curved wooden iron-faced runners, upholstered interior, stenciled decoration - $85

4. Country Baskets

Periodically, a long-neglected artifact of the early American home is discovered. In the 1970's, baskets finally came to the attention of the antique-buying public. A decade ago, country baskets in a variety of shapes and sizes were largely ignored. Prices increased significantly in the early 1970's and have continued to spiral upward.

A critical factor in evaluating an early basket is its condition. A great basket form with gaping holes in the side and bottom is of little value. An example of a damaged rare form may be found in Plate 105. Unlike a piece of furniture, the restoration process in mending the splint and holes does not significantly increase its marketability.

Baskets are still being found in large numbers in antiques shops, attics, barns and at shows. Age of the basket and its original function often are difficult to determine.

The 25% to 50% differential in the price of stoneware, woodenware and furniture prevalent from Maine to California generally is not a factor in the pricing structure of country baskets. The prices asked for early baskets are fairly consistent across the nation.

Splint baskets are still being made by craftsmen in many rural areas and at restorations. These baskets eventually will acquire the patina and wear that will make them appear to be considerably earlier than they are.

The hickory, ash and oak splints used in the early baskets was split from carefully prepared 3″ x 3″ x 3′ strips of wood. The wood was soaked in water for a long time and the bark removed. A froe or special chisel was used to break the strips of wood into $1/8″$ to $1/2″$ splints, up to three feet long.

The cut splints were again soaked to make them pliable for the basket maker.

Plate 76.

Oak splint baskets
Primarily used for storage
c. late 19th century.
Value: $30-$35, $42-$47

Plate 79.

Sewing basket
Probably Shaker, New England, splint and rib
construction, c. 1880.
Value: $90-$110.

Plate 77.

Oak splint work basket
Single-wrapped rim, demi-john or kicked-in bottom,
rib construction, c. mid-1800's.
Value: $85-$100.

This basket form was commonly chosen
for baskets designed to hold sewing tools.

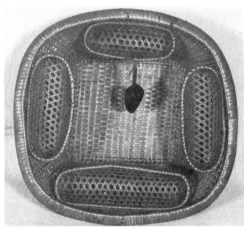

Plate 80.

Sewing basket
Shaker, finely woven, heavily wrapped rim, straw-
berry filled with powdered pumice, c. 1880-1900.
Value: $115-$125.

Plate 78.

Splint work basket
Carved handles, rib construction, c. mid-1800's.
Value: $50-$55.

Sewing baskets and a variety of Victorian
bureau and sewing utensils were produced
and sold in small shops at the New England
Shaker colonies. The Alfred, Maine,
Shakers sold many woven poplar sewing
baskets and pin cushions. The strawberry
contains ground pumice that was ideal for
sharpening needles.

Plate 81.
Bureau box from Alfred, Maine
Shaker, woven poplar, silk lined, front ribbons missing, c. 1880.
Value: $12-$15
    In mint condition with ribbons - $35-$40

Plate 84.
Shaker bureau box
Woven poplar, silk ribbons and interior lining, c. 1880.
Value: $35-$40.

Plate 82.
Shaker trademark stamped on bottom of bureau box
  c. 1880.

Plate 83.
Work basket
Rib construction, single-wrapped rim, carved handles c. mid-1880's.
Value: $60-$70.

This view of the demi-john bottom provides some indication of the skills of the 19th century basket maker who produced this example. A demi-john bottom should add 10% to 20% to the value of a basket.

Plate 85.
White oak splint storage basket
Called an "oriole" basket in Appalachia, dyed splint, c. 1900.
Value: $85-$95.

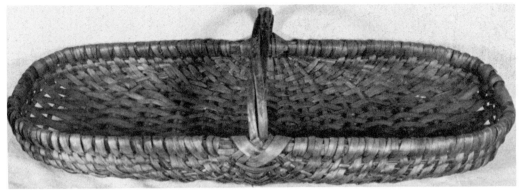

Plate 86.

Splint basket for gathering herbs or flowers
Uncommon twisted handle, shallow, New York state, c. 1870.
Value: $135-$145.

Plate 88.

Willow stick field basket
Crudely constructed, woven willow branches, New York state, c. mid-1800's.
Value: $125-$135.

Plate 87.

Covered buttocks basket
Oak splint, twisted handle, rib construction, 19th century.
Value: $225-$250.

The twisted handle provides an extra degree of strength for carrying heavy loads. This is an uncommon basket form.

A willow stick separated from its bark becomes wicker. In the early 1900's, wicker became very popular for use in summer furniture and baskets. This basket has endured more than a century of hard use. Green willow sticks were wrapped around a pine rib frame and allowed to age gracefully while working in the fields and orchards of New York state.

Plate 89.

Oblong market basket
Shaker, classic handle shape, initialed "W.B.W.",
New England, c. 1850-1860.
Value: $85-$100.

Plate 91.

Oblong market basket
Found in New Hampshire, dyed blue splint, splayed
sides, c. 1870.
Value: $75-$85.

Compare the form of the Shaker baskets
in Plates 89-90 with this basket. As the
interest in Shaker antiques grows, many
items will be mislabeled and sold as Shaker.
Shaker baskets and tinware are difficult to
identify with any degree of certainty, even
by serious collectors.

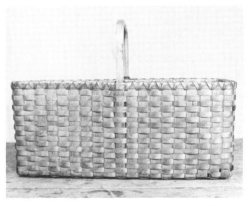

Plate 90.

Oblong market basket
Shaker, note the rim wrap, found near Chatham,
New York, c. 1850-1860.
Value: $100-$115.

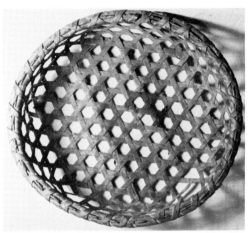

Plate 92.
Rye straw dough basket
Coiled rye straw, banded with hickory or oak splint, probably from Pennsylvania, also called "Mennonite" baskets, c. mid-1800's.
Value: $45-$65.

This bread-raising or dough basket was used in the Mennonite counties of Pennsylvania throughout the 1800's and early 1900's. The top coil was elevated to allow the basket to be hung from a convenient nail. In recent years, rye baskets of questionable age have turned up in many antiques shops. Early baskets should show signs of age, and the splint that binds the rye coils should have developed a patina over time.

Plate 94.
Curd basket
New England, hexagon weave, oak splint, rough condition, c. 1850.
Value: $150-$160.

Cheese or curd baskets were used to separate curds and whey. A piece of cheese cloth was spread in the basket, and the basket was placed on a "cheese ladder" over an open crock. The mixture was poured into the basket and the whey filtered into the crock. The curds were bundled in the cloth and allowed to dry slowly.

Plate 95.
Cheese ladder
New England, mortised and pegged construction, maple, c. 1850.
Value: $50-$60.

Plate 93.
Rye basket with hickory handle
Pennsylvania, c. mid 1800's.
Value: $100-$115.

This example was carefully constructed and artfully designed.

Plate 96.

Cheese ladder
Found in New York state, crudely constructed, pine, c. 1860.
Value: $25-$30.

Plate 98.

Cheese basket (bottom)
Shaker, uncommonly well-made, hickory and ash splint, c. 1850.
Value: $350-$375.

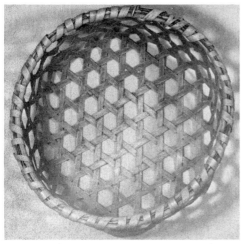

Plate 97.

Cheese basket
New England, 19″ diameter, oak splint, c. 1850.
Value: $250-$275

In 1977 cheese baskets were priced at about $135-$150. In the summer of 1978 a cheese basket would retail for $200-$275 depending upon its construction and condition.

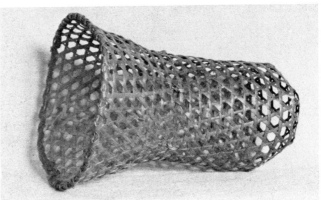

Cheese basket   Plate 99.
New England, rare form, hexagon weave, 5″ diameter x 9″ high, c. 1870.
Value: $165-$175.

Plate 100.

Windsor cheese strainer
New England, maple and ash with hickory rods,
"as found" condition, c. 1820-1830.
Value: $325-$350.

The cheese strainer with attached ladder was used the same as the woven cheese baskets. Windsor or stick construction in this form is rare. The wire repair on the rim does not seriously impair the value of the piece. Early repairs of this type often add to the value of a given piece and make it even more unique.

Plate 101.

Splint field or orchard basket
Oak splint, double-wrapped handles, 42" handle
to handle, New England, c. 1860.
Value: $225-$240.

This basket has survived heavy use in excellent condition. It took a master basket maker using much thickly cut oak splint a long time to produce this uncommon form.

Plate 102.

Large oval field or orchard basket
Single-wrapped rim, inset handles, rib construction,
found in Illinois, c. 1860-1880.
Value: $225-$250.

Open mellon basket
Finely woven splint, rib construction, twisted handle,
c. 1870.
Value: $130-$140.

Field baskets characteristically have an open-plaited bottom that allowed any excess dirt or moisture to escape. It also provided an additional opportunity for air to circulate in a filled basket.

Plate 103.

Field basket
Carved handles, solid sides, thickly cut splint, open plaited bottom, c. 1850.
Value: $225-$250.

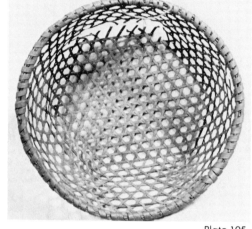

Plate 105.

Kitchen food storage basket
New England Shaker, hexagon open weave, damaged side, c. 1850.
Value: $35-$40.

If this basket were in mint condition, it would be worth $135-$150.

If the basket were skillfully repaired it might increase its value to $70-$75. Perhaps, in time, the scarcity of early forms will increase the value of damaged baskets. At this point, great baskets are still being discovered and collectors have not reached the point where they will pay high prices for broken baskets.

Plate 104.

Field basket
Wrapped rim, oak splint, open plaited bottom, carved handles, c. 1860-1880.
Value: $100-$115.

Plate 106.

Swing-handle basket
Early blue paint, carved bail handle, carved bows, found in Mass., c. 1850.
Value: $225-$250.

Baskets in early paint are rarely found. The value of a basket is increased by 50%-75% if it carries a coat of early blue, red, mustard or green paint. Baskets in white paint are more commonly found than any other color. Their value is raised by 10%-20% over baskets without paint.

The carved bows are fixed to the sides of the basket and allow the handle to swing with a degree of freedom.

Plate 107.

Slide-top basket
Ash splint, early forest green paint, possibly Shaker, bulbous sides, 11½" high from handle to basket bottom, c. 1840.
Value: $110-$140.

Baskets of this form were often used for storing feathers. Typically, they are much larger.

Plate 108.

Swing-handle basket
Ash splint, carved handle and bows, found in New York state, c. 1850.
Value: $125-$150.

Mellon basket

Plate 109.

Splint construction over oak ribs, found in Kentucky, a great worn patina, c. 1860.
Value: $75-$95.

Plate 111.

Crudely-made buttocks basket
Oak splint, rib construction, found in Kentucky, c. 1840.
Value: $50-$75.

Plate 110.

Miniature mellon basket
Rib construction, 6″ diameter, found in Ohio, c. 1870.
Value: $85-$90.

Miniature baskets are not as commonly found as the larger forms.

Plate 112.

Buttocks basket
Found in New York state, unusually finely woven oak splint, c. 1860-1870.
Value: $100-$115.

Plate 113.
Buttocks basket
Oak rib construction, found in Kentucky, c. 1850-1860.
Value: $50-$60.

Plate 115.
Splint basket
Rib construction, double-splint handle, found in Kentucky, c. 1860.
Value: $50-$60.

Plate 114.
Mellon basket
Heavy splint handle, rib construction, oak splint, c. 1850-1860.
Value: $50-$60.

Compare this mellon basket to the buttocks basket in Plate 112. The mellon form has a much less pronounced indentation across the bottom than the buttocks basket. Buttocks baskets appear more often in southern Illinois, Kentucky, Tennessee and West Virginia than in any other section of the country.

Plate 116.
Splint basket
Rib construction, oak splint, c. 1900-1910.
Value: $35-$40.

Many baskets were constructed during a craft revival in the late 1800's and early 1900's. This basket has the added factor of dyed splint to provide a hint of color.

Plate 117.

Hanging storage basket
Crudely-fashioned rib construction, carved handle,
probably European, C. mid-1800's.
Value: $60-$65.

Plate 119.

Hanging basket
Oak splint, rib construction, probably European, c.
mid-1800's.
Value: $50-$55.

Plate 118.

Storage and drying basket
Carved stick handle, rib construction, 4 legs, pos-
sibly European, c. mid-1800's.
Value: $60-$65.

In recent years, a great influx of western
European primitives has disrupted the
antiques market. Many collectors have
purchased Spanish or English iron or furniture under the mistaken impression they
were finding a slice of early America. A
firm in southern New York state has gained
a national reputation for supplying large
quantities of early items from Europe,
Spain and Portugal. Their catalogue is an
excellent investment and education as to
what is currently available. The baskets
in Plates 117-119 have the look of imports.

Basket for carrying two pies
Shaker-made, New England, c. 1890-1900.
Value: $70-$75.

Plate 120.

Plate 122.

Berry basket
5½" from top of handle to bottom, oak splint, New Jersey, c. 1850-1860.
Value: $50-$55.

Plate 121.

Picnic basket
Factory-made, c. 1930.
Value: $15-$20.

Plate 123.

Berry basket
5" high, wooden bottom, iron top and bottom rim, possibly Shaker, c. 1900.
Value: $30-$35.

Plate 124.

Cut-plug tobacco tin
Made to resemble wicker basket, c. 1910.
Value: $20-$25.

Plate 126.

Miniature slide-top basket
Shaker, New England, 5″ from top of handle to bottom, c. 1870.
Value: $70-$80.

Plate 125.

Clam basket in blue paint
Solid ends, pine frame, hickory double-splint handle, Maine, c. 1900-1920.
Value: $65-$75.

Plate 127.

Slide-top basket
Probably Shaker, ash splint, classic handle form, c. 1900.
Value: $70-$75.

Plate 128.

Ash splint field basket
28″ long x 15″ wide, splint handle, Illinois, c. 1870.
Value: $75-$85.

Plate 129.

Field basket
Ash splint, probably Shaker, carved bow handles,
24″ diameter x 20″ high, c. 1870-1880.
Value: $100-$110.

Plate 130.

Lift lid basket
Ash splint, carved handles, possibly Shaker, c. 1870.
Value: $65-$75.

Plate 131.

Miniature mellon basket
Rib construction, excellent patina, New England, c. 1830-1840.
Value: $60-$70.

Plate 132.

Open splint basket
Inset handles, three coats (at least) of early paint, used for storage, c. 1860.
Value: $70-$75.

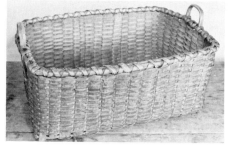

Plate 133.

Field basket
Single-wrapped rim, carved bow handles, open-plaited bottom, oak splint, c. 1850-1870.
Value: $80-$85.

Plate 134.

Shaker washhouse basket
Oak splint, carved bow handles, 16″ high x 18″ x 12″ wide, c. 1850.
Value: $135-$145.

Plate 135.

Algonkian Indian "curly" ornamental basket
Found in northwestern New York state, c. early 1900's.
Value: $25-$35.

Many similar baskets were sold at reservation craft booths and in country stores surrounding eastern Indian reservations.

Plate 136.

Utility basket
Ash splint, carved bow handles, c. 1860-1870.
Value: $55-$65.

Plate 138.

Utility basket
Hickory splint, carved handle, round mouth and square bottom, probably midwestern, c. 1880.
Value: $45-$50.

Plate 137.

Splint flower basket
Thickly cut oak splint, carved handle, used for gathering small flowers, c. 1880.
Value: $50-$55.

Plate 139.

Utility basket
Ash splint, carved handle, round mouth and square bottom, probably midwestern, c. 1880.
Value: $45-$50.

Plate 140.

Utility basket
Carved handle, ash splint, midwestern, c. 1900.
Value: $35-$40.

Plate 142.

Miniature covered basket
Algonkian Indian, New England, 4½″ x 3½″ x 4″, c. 1840.
Value: $85-$95.

The baskets in Plates 138-140 were used for light storage in the kitchen or for gathering enough vegetables for a simple meal from the family garden.

Plate 141.

Algonkian basket
Ash splint, 4″ diameter, every other rib painted, dyed splint, c. 1900.
Value: $30-$35.

Plate 143.

Covered basket
Algonkian Indian, New England, "potato" stamp decoration, c. 1840.
Value: $100-$115.

The Algonkians used a carefully carved potato dipped into a dye or stain made from a combination of fruits and vegetables to produce a simple design on the splint baskets.

Plate 144.

Covered basket
Algonkian Indian, New England, freehand decoration, c. 1840.
Value: $100-$115.

The quality of workmanship in this basket is superior to the more crudely constructed example in Plate 143.

Plate 145.

Covered basket
Algonkian Indian, New England, "potato" stamp decoration, c. 1840.
Value: $100-$115.

The value of the baskets in Plates 142-145 is enhanced because they are part of a graduated "put together" nest of six. A "put together" nest of boxes or baskets is a collection of varying backgrounds but similar forms found over the years and displayed together.

Plate 146.

Storage basket
Ash splint, double-splint bow handles, diameter of 14", single-wrapped rim, c. 1870-1880.
Value: $65-$75.

Plate 147.

Wool drying basket
Pegged frame, four legs, inset handles, New England, c. 1800.
Value: $300-$350.

Plate 148.

Storage basket
Carved bow handles, red and blue dyed hickory splint, probably Indian made, c. 1870.
Value: $65-$75.

Curd or cheese basket
Hexagon weave construction - 26" diameter, New York state, c. 1850.
Value: $250-$275.

Plate 151.

Factory-made wire potato basket
c. 1880-1900.
Value: $45-$55.

Plate 149.

Sweet-grass utility basket
Woven sweet-grass, splint wrapping, Indian made, c. 1850.
Value: $50-$60.
Collection of Mr. & Mrs. Lawrence Hopkins, Bloomington, Ill.

Plate 152.

Factory-made wire egg basket
c. 1880-1900.
Value: $25-$35.

Plate 150.

Algonkian open basket
Blade-ash splint, bow handles, dyed decoration, New England, c. 1840.
Value: $65-$75.

Plate 153.

Plate 154.

Covered basket
Probably Indian-made for the white market, primarily of ash splint, c. 1850.
Value: $75-$85.

The Algonkians and Iroquois made these baskets for whites to use as storage containers for hats and clothing.

Plate 155.

Fruit basket
Ash splint sides, oak splint plaited bottom, inset handles, sployed sides, c. 1860.
Value: $55-$60.

This early form of the berry basket preceeded the mass-produced pine and basswood containers that became popular after 1865.

Preliminary Quiz II

1. The handle of this basket is:
   a. fixed
   b. a slide top
   c. a bale type
   d. none of the above

2. True   False   This is an example of a basket that was made with rib construction.

3. What is the approximate value of this basket?
   a. less than $25
   b. $50-$75
   c. $100-$125
   d. more than $150

Answers may be found on page 164.

5. Country Pottery

Decorated stoneware pottery prices vary widely in antiques shops across the country. Prices are a minimum of 25% to 30% lower on the east coast, and increase proportionately as one heads west. A standard "bird" jug in New York state and New England may be purchased for $90 to $140, depending upon size, condition and the pottery where it was made. In the middle-west, the same decorated jug probably would sell for $130-$185. This price differentiation is due to the scarcity of decorated stoneware made in midwestern potteries. The vast majority of the stoneware turned out in Illinois, Missouri and points west was undecorated or contained simple swirls of cobalt decoration or numbers. Many of these pieces of late stoneware were quickly and simply decorated with a stencil.

New York state and New England stoneware that does not have the name of the specific pottery impressed into the neck of the piece generally is worth 10% to 15% less than signed examples. Stoneware from the Bennington, Vermont, pottery is especially popular in the midwest and west and commands even higher prices. Bennington stoneware is more valuable not because of its quality, but due to a mystique that has developed over the years. A Bennington "bird" jug is often 15% to 20% more expensive than a similar example from Whites' Utica or Fort Edward, New York.

The value of a piece of post-1850 stoneware is generally determined by the decoration it carries. The more heavily painted with deep cobalt, the more valuable the piece.

Standard decorations include swirls, flowers, insects and numbers. A crock or jug with humans, lions, deer, ships or buildings in cobalt are rare and expensive. Often, these are advertised for $500 to $3,000, depending on the complexity of the decoration and the pottery where it was produced.

Plate 157.

2-gallon stoneware jug
No decoration, ovoid form, c. 1830-1840.
Value: $85-$100.

Plate 156.

3-gallon redware jug
Incised "3", swirl of cobalt, ovoid form, New England, c. 1830.
Value: $200-$225.

The earliest form that American pottery took is illustrated in Plate 5. Ovoid jugs are uncommon and seldom decorated. Incising was a process of scratching a design into the damp surface of a freshly turned piece with a thin slice of sharpened iron.

Plate 158.

2-gallon stoneware crock
Cobalt blue floral spray, impressed "FB Norton & Co., Worcester, Mass", c. 1870-1875.
Value: $95-$115.

Compare the later impressed "2" with the early incised "3" on the ovoid jug in Plate 156.

Plate 159.

E. and L.P. Norton 4-gallon jug
Bennington, Vermont, cobalt floral spray, c. 1861-1881.
Value: $125-$140.

5-gallon "bird" jug
Gately, Boston, Mass., well-defined "fat" robin, c. 1870.
Value: $150-$200.

Plate 160.

3-gallon "bird" crock
Scatterlee and Mory, Fort Edward, New York, c. 1870.
Value: $140-$180.

Five and six-gallon decorated jugs appear less often than do the more commonly found 1½-3 gallon examples.

Plate 161.

4-gallon "bird" crock
Ottman Bros., Fort Edward, New York, c. 1875.
Value: $150-$180.

Plate 162.

Decorated preserve jar
Cowden and Wilcox, Harrisburg, PA, vine and cobalt grapes, c. 1870-1875.
Value: $150-$200.

In 1862, the Ballard Pottery of Burlington, Vermont, listed four-gallon decorated preserve jars with lids for $9 a dozen. The 1½-gallon jars were offered at $5 a dozen.

Plate 165.

Decorated stoneware preserve jar
Slip cup bird in cobalt, impressed "C.W. Braun,
Buffalo", c. 1865-1870.
Value: $175-$185.

Plate 163.

Batter jug
Unsigned, Albany slip decoration over stoneware,
original tin covers, c. 1880.
Value: $100-$125.

In 1899, a Syracuse, New York, pottery
was selling similar 1½-gallon jugs with
tin covers for $4 a dozen.

A slip cup was a pottery decorating tool
used much like a cake decorator to spread
a thin line of cobalt blue slip. Stoneware
with slip cup decoration is less commonly
found than brush decorated stoneware. A
comparison may be made between the slip
cup bird on the Braun jar and the brush
decorated bird on the five-gallon jug at
right.

Plate 164.

Decorated 4-gallon "bird" crock
Unsigned, found in New York state, c. 1870-1875.
Value: $150-$175.

Plate 166.

3-gallon "bird" jar
Whites' Utica, originally had a tin lid and bale
handle, c. 1875.
Value: $150-$170.

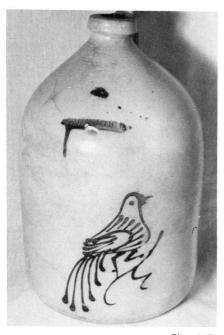

Plate 167.
Whites' Utica 3-gallon "bird" jug
Splash of cobalt over impressed signature, c. 1870-1875.
Value: $150-$175.

Plate 168.
N.A. White and Son 2-gallon crock
c. 1850.
Value: $150-$160.

Heavily decorated crocks of deep cobalt are uncommon. The cobalt became so expensive that it was necessary for the potteries to water down the slip to make it go farther.

Plate 169.
1½-gallon crock from the New York Stoneware Company
Cobalt horse fly decoration, impressed "6", c. 1870.
Value: $100-$115.

(Caraker Collection)

The impressed "6" probably indicates the size in a series that the pottery made, rather than the number of gallons it held. The horse fly was put on with a slip cup.

Plate 170.
Unsigned 6-gallon "bird" crock
Combination of brush and slip cup decoration, c. 1860.
Value: $200-$225.

Plate 172.

Six-gallon crock
Heavily decorated cobalt bird, F.B. Norton, Worcester, Mass., c. 1870.
Value: $250-$300.

Plate 171.
Uncommon 4-gallon "duck" crock
W. Hart, Ogdensburgh, rare form for a "bird", c. 1860.
Value: $250-$275.

The standard cobalt bird found on most crocks or jugs appears in Plates 160-161. This example took more of a whimsical attitude or a degree of creativity to develop.

After the late-1870's, relatively few heavily decorated pieces of stoneware were created. A network of roads and railways opened up previously captured markets to nation-wide distribution of goods. The increased costs of labor and competition forced the potteries to produce stoneware as cheaply as possible and provide decoration only on special order at an increased cost.

Plate 173.
2-gallon jar
Lyons, New York state, heavy cobalt flower, applied ear handles, c. 1860.
Value: $125-$135.

Plate 174.

Stoneware jar
J. Norton, Bennington, Vermont, 1½-gallon, deep cobalt bird, c. 1859-1861.
Value: $150-$180.

Bennington pottery is relatively easy to date by the impressed signature. J. Norton and Co. operated the pottery between 1859 and 1861. The longest period of ownership was between 1861 and 1881 with the E. and L. P. Norton mark. The value of Bennington stoneware is significantly affected by the impressed mark. The largest period of production and the most common mark is the E. and L. P. Norton.

Plate 175.

Bennington two-gallon jug
E. and L. P. Norton, Bennington, Vermont, simple deep blue cobalt flower, c. 1861-1881.
Value: $75-$100.

Plate 176.

2-gallon jug
Unmarked, probably White's Utica, interesting flower, c. 1870.
Value: $100-$110.

Plate 177.

2-gallon stoneware jar
Brush decoration, blue "2", c. 1850.
Value: $85-$95.

Plate 179.
Butter crock
Applied ear handles, cobalt decoration, original
lid, brushwork decoration, c. 1860.
Value: $175-$225.

Plate 178.
4-gallon Peoria Pottery crock
Albany slip decoration, molded rather than hand-
thrown, c. 1880-1890.
Value: $55-$70.

Peoria Pottery is considerably more valuable in Peoria County, Illinois, than in any
other area of the nation. Many other late
examples from local potteries are eagerly
sought in a limited geographic area, and
hardly recognized in the rest of the country.
Peoria pottery is interesting because Chris-
topher Fenton of Bennington, Vermont,
and the legendary pottery there helped to
establish the Illinois pottery.

Plate 180.
Late 2-gallon midwestern jug
Buff color, cylindrical sides, no decoration, c. 1900
Value: $12-$15.

Butter crocks in original condition are
difficult to find with an original lid. A collector should check the lid to make sure
it has not been a recent addition. The
glazes, decoration and wear on the crock
and lid should match.

Compare the jugs in Plates 156 and 157
with this jug. Note how the ovoid or pear
shape has been transformed over about 75
years to a cylindrical form. It is possible
to judge the relative age of a piece of stoneware by the degree to which the piece is
caught between the ovoid and cylindrical
form. It was a gradual change and much
can be learned by careful study.

Plate 181.
1-gallon jug
Deep cobalt decoration, c. 1875-1880.
Value: $60-$70.

Plate 182.
2-gallon jug
Impressed, "2", cobalt flower, c. 1870-1875.
Value: $70-$75.

Plate 183.
3-gallon stoneware churn
Midwest, late swirl decoration, c. 1880-1890.
Value: $85-$95.

The wooden dasher and lid are original to the churn. Churns of this type were made well into the 1900's. The swirl decoration and hastily drawn "3" are indicative of the dying days of decorative stoneware.

Plate 184.
Molded stoneware bottle
Splash of cobalt on the neck, marked "Green and Clark", c. 1880.
Value: $25-$30.

Plate 185.

Stoneware spittoon
Unsigned, brushwork decoration, c. 1850.
Value: $130-$140.

Spittoons were in the precarious position of being constantly underfoot. They were stepped on, kicked and periodically cleaned. It is not surprising that few have survived.

Plate 186.

Stonewar jar
Applied ear handles, unsigned, probably made in New York state, c. 1860-1870.
Value: $90-$100.

Many pieces of stoneware carry a cobalt decoration that is difficult to specifically identify. This particular example could be a variety of things. If it were a side view of a man with his arm cocked in a throwing position it would certainly be rare.

Plate 187.

Stenciled jug
Hamilton and Jones, Greensboro, PA., c. 1865-1870.
Value: $65-$75.

Stenciling initially became popular in the early 1850's when the competition between potteries forced a quicker means of decorating stoneware. Some magnificent examples of Hamilton and Jones stoneware are occasionally found that combine stenciling with elaborate brush work.

Plate 188.

Stoneware preserve jar.
Unmarked, probably midwestern, c. 1875-1880.
Value: $20-$25.

Plate 189.

Redware pitcher
Found in southern Illinois, unmarked, c. 1830-1840.
Value: $50-$60.

Plate 191.

Redware jar
Unmarked, c. 1830.
Value: $60-$65.

Plate 190.

Redware jar
Unmarked, found in Pennsylvania, c. 1840.
Value: $40-$45.

A redware pie plate or serving plate that has its surface decorated with a word or phrase written in slip is worth three to five times a conventional undecorated plate. Pie plates were glazed and decorated only on the inside surface. The pie was removed from the plate in which it was baked before it was cut and served.

The first pottery produced in America was made from the red clay that was available in vast quantities along the eastern seaboard. The redware pottery was fired at relatively low temperatures that produced a brittle product. Because of its inability to be water tight, it was necessary to seal or glaze the redware.

Plate 192.

Redware pie plate
8″ diameter, heavily carboned bottom, found in Ohio, glazed interior, c. 1820.
Value: $65-$75.

Plate 193.

Redware apple butter pot
Unmarked, glazed interior, found in Pennsylvania, c. 1840.
Value: $85-$95.

Plate 195.

Redware pots
Incised lines, found in Pennsylvania, unmarked, glazed interiors, c. 1840.
Value: $60-$65.

The only decoration on this pot is the incised lines on the shoulder or upper portion. This pot was used to serve apple butter at the dinner table. Pots used for storage were made without handles.

Plate 194.

Redware milk pan
10″ diameter, found in Pennsylvania, unmarked, c. 1840.
Value: $100-$110.

Plate 196.

Apple butter pot
Green glaze, found in Ohio, unmarked, for table use, c. 1830-1840.
Value: $135-$150.

A potter had a variety of glaze colorings from which to choose, including black, red, orange, brown and yellow. The green glaze was made from oxidized copper that was expensive and often difficult to obtain.

Plate 199.

Yellow-ware mixing bowl
8″ diameter, molded, c. 1900.
Value: $20-$25.

Plate 197.

Redware preserve jar
Deep brown glaze, found in Ohio, unmarked, c. 1840-1850.
Value: $50-$55.

Yellow-ware is found with decorative bands of blue, white, black or brown.

Plate 200.

Stoneware inkwell
Glazed, unsigned, pierced for 3 quill pens, recessed dipping well, c. 1840.
Value: $50-$60.

Plate 198.

Yellow-ware mixing bowl
9″ diameter, molded, unmarked, c. 1900.
Value: $20-$25.

Yellow-ware was a popular item in the mail order catalogs of the late 1800's and early 1900's. The pottery was molded rather than hand thrown and available in sets of varying size.

Plate 201.

Stoneware cream pitcher
5″ high, held less than a pint, unsigned, dark exterior glaze, c. 1870.
Value: $45-$55.

Plate 202.

Stoneware jar
Incised lines, unsigned, c. 1880.
Value: $35-$45.

Plate 203.

Redware pie plates
8″ diameter, unsigned, coggled edges, unglazed bottoms.
Value: $55-$65.

Preliminary Quiz III

1. The approximate value of this 5-gallon crock is:
   a. $50-$75
   b. $80-$110
   c. $115-$130
   d. more than $140

2. What would be the approximate value of the crock without the cobalt bird?
   a. $25 or less
   b. $40-$50
   c. $75-$85
   d. more than $100

3. True   False   This crock would date from approximately 1900-1910.

Answers may be found on page 164.

Prices of Pottery Advertised in 1973

When we began this project we decided it was equally as important to have an understanding of prices in the recent past as it is to be aware of the current market trends. In the early 1970's, stoneware escalated dramatically in value at auctions and antiques shows. We have gathered the descriptions and asking prices of 15 unusual pieces of decorated stoneware that were advertised in 1973.

1. 2-gal. Whites' Utica "bird" crock - fan tail bird perched on branches - $85
2. 3-gal crock - Warner, West Troy, N.Y. - large flying eagle with banners in its beak - $325
3. 1-gal. jug - signed "Boston" - decorated with a brushed large cod fish - $500
4. 4-gal crock - Ottman Bros., Ft. Edward, N.Y. - large basket filled with fruit in cobalt - $300
5. 2-gal jug - large urn-shaped vase with a bouquet of flowers - missing handle - $300
6. 1½-gal. crock - detailed bird on a branch - Underwood, Ft. Edward - $65

7. 2-gal. crock - incised bird on front and back - ears have broken off - $1,000
8. Preserve jar - Bell, Cornwall, N.Y. - impressed "1" with impressed leaves around it - $50
9. Flask - 8" tall - unmarked - $35
10. 3-gal. crock - human hand forming the "O.K." sign - West Troy, N.Y. - $385
11. 4-gal. crock - large 5-pointed star - "4" on reverse side - $300
12. 2-gal. jug - E. and L. P. Norton - highly stylized flower - $65
13. 2-gal. jug - Smith and Day, Norwalk, Conn. - ovoid - brush decoration across name - $65
14. 3-gal. churn - Whites' Utica - four 1" brushed bands - $100
15. 2-gal. crock - semi-ovoid - "Pottery Works" - two brushed leaves - $90

After studying the 15 pieces of stoneware described above and reflecting upon the current prices that follow, it appears to us that stoneware has risen as much over the last five years as other areas of country antiques.

Variety of tins, $5-$30
Yellow-ware bowls, $15-$25
Glass bottles, $12-$16

Variety of late 19th Century quilts, $125-$225

New York state stoneware, $60-$175

Candlemolds, $45-$75
Hog scraper candlesticks, $45-$165
Tray and candle snuffer, $50
Grained blanket chest, $200-$225

Coverlet dated 1836, $350-$375
Brass warming pan, $275-$285
Brass andirons, $300-$325

Tiger maple boot jacks, $35-$45
Baskets, $45-$100
Redware jar, $65-$75

Treen sugar bowl, $250
Child's tiger maple tea table, $75-$85

Pewter candlesticks, $175-$185
Pewter charger, $100-$125
Tiger maple noggin, $250-$275
Tiger maple rolling pin, $60-$75

Chest of drawers, c. 1820, $650-$675
Iron peel, $65-$70
Foot warmer, $85-$100
High chair, $200-$225

Rockingham pie plates, $55-$60
Bowls, $35-$50
Pantry boxes, $40-$50

Large pewter teapot, $525-$550
Country Queen Anne chair, $350-$400
Bucket bench, $350-$375

Hanging candle box in old red, $250-$265
Set of 6 Rhode Island Windsor chairs, $4,000-$5,000
William and Mary gateleg table, $2,400-$2,600

Copper and brass warming pans, $300-$350
Andirons, $150-$175
Windsor arm chair, $850-$950
Tilt-top stand, $450-$550

Country Queen Anne tea table, $600-$675
Cone-base candleholder, $175-$200
Queen Anne bannister-back chair, $350-$425

New York state coverlet, c. 1840, $175-$200
Mocha ware, c. 1830, $65-$150

Painted tin or tole ware, document boxes and trays, $45-$150.

Selected 1977 Stoneware Prices from Garth's Auction

1. Stoneware jug - blue transfer label - "Casey Bros., Scranton, PA." and "Pasteur Chamberland Filter Co. Dayton, Ohio" - 7½" - $27.50
2. Stoneware bottle - "Vimo, Ginger Beer, Cleveland, O." - 6½" high - $11
3. Stoneware flask - 8" high - $37.50
4. 6-gallon stoneware double-handled jar - signature in cobalt - "Lampert, Wenport" - 19" high - $37.50
5. Stoneware jar - simple leaf in cobalt - 10¼" high - $27.50
6. 4-gal. butter crock - impressed signature - "A.O. Whittemore, Havana, N.Y." - well-drawn bird in cobalt - $200
7. 2-gal jug - "J. and E. Norton, Bennington, Vt." - swirled design in cobalt - $135
8. 2-gal. ovoid jug - "I. M. Mead" - brushed cobalt flower - $105
9. 3-gal. stoneware jug - "3" in cobalt - 14½" h. - $17.50
10. Miniature stoneware advertising jug - incised label - "Husch Bros., Louisville, Ky." - 3" high - $14
11. 4-gal. stoneware jar - stenciled label - "William and Reppert, Greensboro, Pa." - 14" high - $27.50
12. 6-gal. stoneware jug - cobalt label - "Grant and Colfax 1868" - 16½" high - $95
13. Stoneware jar - stenciled cobalt label - "T. F. Reppert, Greensboro, Pa." - 9¾" h. - $32.50
14. Stoneware jar - stenciled label - "Hamilton and Jones, Greensboro, Pa." - 8" high - $45
15. Redware plate - 4-line yellow slip decoration with green - coggled edge - mint - 11½" d. - $375
16. Redware pitcher - greenish tan glaze - 7¾" high - $15
17. Redware plate - yellow slip design with splashes of green and a clear shiny glaze - 8" diameter - $100
18. Stoneware batter pitcher - Albany slip - exterior has worn painted flower - 7¾" h. - $2
19. Stoneware jug - impressed signature "N.Y. Stoneware Company" - simple cobalt leaf design - 14" h. - $37.50
20. 2-gal. stoneware batter pitcher - "E. Bishop, near Burlington, Ohio" - blue brushed design at spout - 13½" - $75
21. 3-gal. jar - "E. A. Montell, Olean, N.Y." - brushed cobalt flower - 10¾" h. - $65
22. 3-gal. stoneware jar - "T. Reed" - brushed cobalt tulip - 11½" h. - $195
23. Stoneware canning jar - cobalt blue brushed designs - 9½" h. - $70
24. 2-gal. batter pitcher - flower and squiggly lines with "1843" in cobalt slip - 13¾" h. - $280
25. 10-gal. stoneware crock - comic drawing of old woman with curly hair in cobalt slip - 13½" d. x 17¼" h. - $595
26. 6-gal. stoneware crock - incised cow - blue cobalt - "Gardiner Stone Ware, Manufactory, Gardiner, Me." - $55
27. 3-gal. stoneware ovoid jug - cobalt blue brushed on at handle - 16¾" h. - $45
28. Stoneware batter pitcher - brush floral design in cobalt blue - $300
29. Bennington covered jar - "1849" mark - $265
30. Stoneware "bird" crock - "New York Stoneware Co. North Edward N.Y. 6" - modern wooden lid - 8" h. - $105
31. 5-gal. crock - three incised eagles, each with spear and banner - 12" h. - $85
32. Stoneware butter crock - brushed blue feather designs - 8½" d. - $165
33. 3-gal. crock - hen pecking corn in cobalt - 10½" h. - $165
34. Small wooden washboard - redware insert in wooden frame 7" x 13½" - $37.50
35. Stoneware jar - applied handles - brushed blue floral band - 13½" h. - $95
36. 5-gallon stoneware jug - "Weading and Belding, Brantford, Ohio" - brushed flower - 18½" h. - $65
37. 3-gal. stoneware crock - gilt-work decoration - 13½" h. - $75

20 Pieces of Pottery Advertised in 1977

The following examples of country pottery were advertised by antiques dealers across the country during 1977.

1. 4-gal. Bennington jug with 2 cobalt birds - $220 - New Hampshire dealer
2. Ovoid jug - ring neck - "Orcutt and Waite/ Whately" - mint - $95 - N.Y. dealer
3. Cobalt blue fish on H.D. Whittemore, Havana N.Y., crock - $750 - N.Y. dealer
4. Bennington cuspidor (spittoon) - $35 - N.H. dealer
5. Bennington wood and stoneware - glazed wash board - Mass. dealer - $400
6. 1-gal. crock with cobalt spotted sand piper - Hartford, Conn. - N.Y. dealer - $295
7. 1-gal. stoneware jar - eagle holding arrows behind a shield - $325 - N.Y. dealer
8. W. Hart - 4-gal. crock with horse's head in cobalt - $275 - Ontario, Canada, show
9. Green spongeware bowl - 9" diameter - $65 - N.H. dealer
10. J. and E. Horton 1-gal. jug with cobalt swirl decoration - $65 - Texas dealer
11. Paul Cushman - 1-gal. jar - sealed crock - $165 - Mass. dealer
12. C. Crolins, Manhattan Wells - incised - 2-gal. jug - 13½" h. - $795 - Mass. dealer
13. JA and CW Underwood, Ft. Edward, N.Y. - 1-gal. jug with floral cobalt - $60 - N.Y. dealer
14. J. Norton and Son, Bennington, Vt. - ovoid o-gal. jar - ochre moth decoration - $475 - N.Y. dealer
15. Bennington-type cuspidor - signed "Sharpe" - $28 - Mass. dealer
16. Stoneware bottle - no markings - tan - $9.50 - Maine dealer
17. 3-gal. Ft. Edward, N.Y. - "bird" jug - $80 - New Hampshire dealer
18. Crock - incised eagle and swan - $135 - New Jersey dealer
19. A.K. Ballard, Burlington, Vermont - 2-gal. jug - $50 - N.H. dealer
20. 2-gal. container - incised "Ice Water" - blue flowers and brass spigot - $195 - N.H. dealer

July 1977 Auction Prices of Pottery

Some excellent insights into the stoneware market can be made by studying the results of an auction in Duncansville, Pennsylvania, in July, 1977.

The following items were especially noteworthy among the more than 400 pieces of stoneware sold at the third annual auction:

1. John Burger, Rochester - 6-gal. crock - large elk with two trees in deep cobalt - with two large cracks - $950
2. 6-gallon jar - brushed cobalt decoration of blue morning glories above two women and a small child, all within an open wreath - $1,350
3. A. O. Whittemore - 4-gal. crock - Havana, N.Y. - small cobalt house with five windows and two chimneys surrounded by weeds - $550
4. West Troy, N.Y. - 5-gal. crock - large dog in cobalt in front of a fence - $800
5. S. Skinner and Co., Picton, C.W. - 3-gal. jar - cobalt bird with fish in its mouth - $550
6. 2-gal. jug - Ottman Bros. and Co., Fort Edward, N.Y. - cobalt longnosed man seated on a keg drinking from a bottle under "CENTENNIAL" - $925
7. Hamilton and Jones - Greensboro, Oa. - 4 gal. jar - heavily stenciled - 14¼" high - $75
8. 14" high ovoid jug - crudely drawn running rabbit - $275
9. "M.A. Ingalls, Liquor Dealer, Little Falls," 2 strap handles, 5 gallons - $50
10. 3 gal. crock - chicken pecking corn in cobalt blue, 10½" high - $230
11. Cowden and Wilcox "Man in the Moon" jar - $500
12. 1 gal. "bird" decorated batter jar - minus tin spout caps and bale handle, repaired ear - $120

6. Kitchen and Hearth Antiques

Rural America was basically a hand-crafted society until the mid-1800's when industrialization and mass production began to affect the tastes of the American family.

The first 250 years of colonization, revolution and immigration before 1850 found the kitchen and hearth tools used in cooking produced by a local blacksmith, a tinsmith or a husband handy with a carving knife and a supply of pine and maple.

Stores came to even the remotest village after the mid-point of the 19th century with large supplies of factory-made hardware, stoves, buckets, table ware and packaged groceries.

It is increasingly difficult for collectors today to find early woodenware and iron cooking utensils. In the late 1960's, the problem was compounded by a large influx of wooden spoons, stools, baskets, food molds, buckets and a wide variety of early iron from Spain, Portugal, Eastern Europe and Mexico.

These imports were brought into the United States in such large quantities and offered at such reasonable prices that a number of obvious problems were created for collectors of American kitchen antiques. It might be wise for collectors to obtain a copy of the importers' catalogs and learn the hearth and kitchen items available.

Kitchen pieces in metal, wood or pottery have more of a standard nationwide value than early furniture. They are easier to use in the Kansas split-level than a high-back dry sink in early worn paint, and certainly easier to transport from Vermont or New Hampshire. Many collectors become interested at a point in their lives when they have already furnished their homes and have room only for decorative accessories.

Plate 206.

Maple bowl
Hand-hewn maple, c. 1840.
Value: $75-$85

Plate 204.
Nest of pantry boxes
Early original paint, round boxes, excellent condition, c. 1880.
Value: $35-$45 each, $280-$300 for the nest.

In the past few years pantry boxes have been "discovered" and prices have soared. Painted boxes are at least 40% to 50% more expensive than refinished or unpainted boxes. The nests or stocks that collectors build are "put together." An original nest in old paint is almost impossible to obtain.

Plate 207.
Chopping bowl
Maple, early blue paint in worn condition, c. 1860-65.
Value: $75-$85.

Plate 205.
Scouring box
Box, scouring board, tin pumice holder, c. 1860-1870.
Value: $50-$55.

A scouring box was used to sharpen knives. Pumice was placed on the surface of the board and knives were rubbed on the pumice.

Plate 208.
Chopping bowl
Found in Kentucky, pine, "as found" condition, c. 1850.
Value: $45-$50.

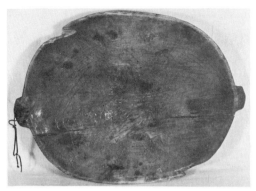

Plate 209.

Chopping bowl
Maple, early form, "ear" handles, c. 1830.
Value: $80-$85.

Plate 212.

Burl bowl
Found in New England - 14" diameter, c. 1830-1850.
Value: $425-$450.

Plate 210.

Work bowl
Maple, 38" long x 20", hand-hewn, c. 1850.
Value: $125-$135.

Plate 213.

Burl butter worker, hand-formed.
Found in New England, c. 1830.
Value: $150-$165.

Plate 211.

Chopping board
Pine, "as found" condition, difficult to date.
Value: $40-$50.

Pieces that have had heavy use are difficult to date accurately. Chopping boards in this form were in use throughout the 19th century and well into the 20th century.

Plate 214.

Butter worker
Tiger maple, hand-formed, c. 1840.
Value: $75-$85.

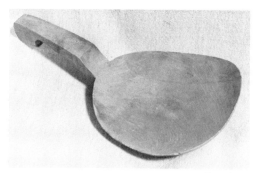

Plate 215.

Butter worker "blank"
Maple, machine-formed, c. 1880-1900.
Value: $15-$20.

Butter workers were used to "work" or press excess water out of freshly churned butter. Like many factory-made pieces of wooden ware, this butter worker was roughed out on a machine. Unlike other factory-made workers, this example was never finished. It was stored with thousands of others when the factory closed. For many years a New York state relative of the owner used the "blanks" as kindling for fires on long cold evenings. Several years ago, the few remaining pieces were salvaged by a prominent eastern dealer.

Plate 217.

Pantry boxes
Early paint, nailed joints, 6" d. and 7" d., c. 1880.
Value: $40-$50.

Plate 216.

Peel
Pine, found in Ohio, used to remove baked goods from oven, c. 1860-1870.
Value: $30-$40.

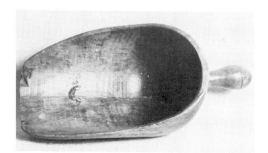

Plate 218.

Scoop
Maple, formed from single piece of wood, used with flour or sugar, c. 1870.
Value: $75-$85.

Plate 221.

Miniature cookie cutter
Tin heart, maple handle, found in southern New York state, 1½" h. x 2" d., c. 1830-1840.
Value: $115-$125.

Plate 219.

Butter worker
Maple, factory-made, c. 1870.
Value: $18-$25.

Plate 222.

Potato masher
Maple, factory-made, c. 1900.
Value: $10-$12.

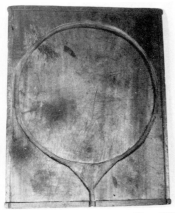

Plate 220.

Cheese draining board
Maple, bread board ends, homemade, c. 1860.
Value: $110-$115.

Bread board ends are the two strips of wood nailed to the top and bottom of the cheese drainer to keep it from warping. They are also commonly found on tables and chopping boards.

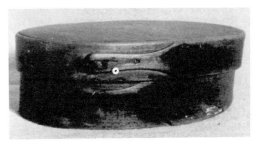

Plate 223.

Oval pantry box
Maple sides and pine top, finger lap construction, original finish, c. 1830-1840.
Value: $40-$45.

Compare the finger laps on this colonist or pantry box with several of the Shaker oval boxes in Section 8.

Plate 224.

Butter mold
Maple, hand-carved leaf design, c. 1850.
Value: $65-$70.

Plate 226.

Butter print
Maple, possibly English, rare "bird" print, c. 1870-1880.
Value: $175-$200.

Plate 225.

Butter mold
Machine-made cow, maple, c. 1870-1880.
Value: $145-$160.

Plate 227.

Butter mold
Machine-carved leaves and strawberry, maple, c. 1880.
Value: $65-$85.

The value of a butter print or mold is largely determined by the design it carries. Animals and birds are difficult to find and expensive to buy. The more commonly found designs include leaves, flowers, wheat or geometric patterns.

The wooden mold that shapes the butter is called a bell or beehive. After the butter was packed into the bell, the plunger was pushed and the butter emerged onto a plate with a form and a decorative design.

Plate 230.

Butter mold
Maple, machine-made, floral decoration, rare form, c. 1870-1875.
Value: $200-$225.

Plate 228.

Butter print
Rare American eagle, maple, machine-carved, c. 1860-1865.
Value: $200-$225.

The prints or stamps were turned on a lathe and the design was pressed into the maple surface by a machine. Prior to the pressing process the maple was steamed. In recent years, this particular design has been reproduced in large quantities.

Plate 231.

Butter print
Maple, machine-made, c. 1875-1880.
Value: $40-$45.

Butter prints are commonly found in wood, although examples in tin, redware and ironstone are known. The authors have owned a butter mold with a tin bell or beehive and maple plunger and stamp.

Plate 229.

Butter print
Maple, wheat design, hand-carved, c. 1860.
Value: $70-$75.

Plate 232.

Maple butter print
Hand-carved, geometric patterns, figures and numbers, c. 1840-1850.
Value: $100-$125.

Plate 233.

Mortar and pestle

Maple, incised lines, original unpainted condition, c. 1850.

Value: $70-$75.

Plate 235.

Mortar and pestle

Deep green paint, maple, c. 1850-1860.

Value: $75-$85.

Mortars and pestles were popular in early kitchens for grinding spices, herbs and home produced medicinal compounds. The interior of a mortar should show much wear and signs of heavy use. Many times the mortar and pestle became separated over the years and a substitute pestle was provided.

Plate 234.

Mortar and pestle

Maple, early green paint, c. 1840-1850.

Value: $75-$85.

Plate 236.

Mortar and pestle

Original early condition, decorative lines on mortar, c. 1850.

Value: $60-$65.

Plate 237.

Mortar and pestle
Maple, decoratives lines on mortar and pestle, c.
1850-1860.
Value: $60-$65.

Plate 239.

Wooden funnel
Maple, original condition, c. 1860.
Value: $75-$85.

Funnels were made of papier-mache,
wood, copper and ironstone.

Plate 238.

Wooden funnel
Maple, refinished, great early repair on lip, c. 1860.
Value: $75-$85.

Plate 240.

Staved bucket
Early blue-green paint, button hoops, c. 1850.
Value: $65-$85.

Plate 241.

Sugar bucket
Also called a firkin, refinished, staved, swing handle,
copper nails and bands, c. 1880.
Value: $70.-$80.

Plate 242.

Sugar bucket
Ash and maple, staved construction, swing handle,
refinished, c. 1880.
Value: $60-$70.

Sugar buckets or firkins in original paint
are worth 40% to 50% more than the refinished examples.

Plate 243.

Lid from sugar bucket in Plate 242
Signed "D. Wilder and Son" from Mass., c. 1880.

This bucket is "signed" only to the extent
that the name of the factory in which it
was produced is impressed into the lid.

In many antiques shops this adds another
10% to 15% to the value. When the term
"signed" is used accurately, it normally
refers to a signature or wood burn on the
bottom of an early Windsor chair.

Plate 244.

Miniature firkin
6" diameter x 8" high, maple and ash, swing handle,
c. 1900-1915.
Value: $45-$60.

Plate 245.
Painted firkin or sugar bucket
Staved, wooden bands, swing handle, c. 1870.
Value: $85-$100.

Plate 247.
Painted bucket
10" diameter x 6" high, staved, red paint, iron bands, c. 1860-1870.
Value: $50-$55.

Another $10-$15 would be added to the piece if it carried early blue paint rather than red or yellow.

Plate 246.
Milk bucket
Blue-green paint, Lancaster, Pa., dairy, staved, iron bands, c. early 20th century.
Value: $60-$85.

Plate 248.
Early rain barrel
2" thick pine staves, hand wrought iron bands, c. 1830.
Value: $100-$125.

Plate 249.

Wooden salt box
Pine staves, hickory bands, red and blue paint,
c. 1820-1830.
Value: $125-$150.

A close look at the upper band suggests
that it might be an early replacement.
Seldom does an early piece make it through
150 years without a legitimate replacement
or three.

Plate 251.

Candle box
Slide top, box from single piece of wood, nautical
or marine carvings, c. 1820.
Value: $220-$240.

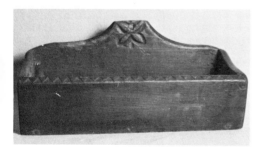

Plate 250.

Hanging candle box
Early blue-green paint, pine, c. mid-1800's.
Value: $130-$150.

Plate 252.

Knife box
Early green paint, slide top, carved finger pull, c.
1870-1880.
Value: $60-$80.

Plate 253.

Turned wood bowl
Red paint, 4″ diameter, maple, c. 1860.
Value: $45-$55.

Four cream skimmers and two small plates
Maple, obvious milk odor, c. 1840
Value: $18-$22 each

Plate 255.

Scrubbing board
Factory-made, child's size, c. 1920-1930.
Value: $25-$35.

Plate 254.

Scrubbing board
Hand hewn, separate area at top for soap, c. 1830.
Value: $115-$125.

Plate 256.

Maple bowl
14½″ diameter, warped, early green paint, c. 1860.
Value: $95-$105.

Plate 257.

Knife and fork box
Splayed sides, nailed rather than dovetailed, walnut,
c. 1860-1870.
Value: $45-$50.

Plate 259.

Dough trough
Cherry, early paint, inset handles, wide dovetails,
c. late 18th century.
Value: $150-$160.

Plate 258.
Dasher butter churn
Staved, iron bands, c. 1840.
Value: $175-$200.

Plate 260.
Decorated tray
Maple, pine bottom, possibly Scandinavian, 14″
diameter, c. 1850.
Value: $130-$135.

Plate 261.

Bride's box
"As found" condition, oval, possibly Scandinavian,
c. 1850.
Value: $70-$75.

Plate 262.

Plate 263.

Turned salt bowl
Maple, found in New York state, c. 1860.
Value: $85-$95.

Sander
Maple, lathe-turned, New York state, c. 1840.
Value: $40-$45.

Plate 264.

Serving tray
Pine, early paint, probably used in tavern, c. 1840.
Value: $75-$85.

Plate 265.

Wooden clothes ringer
C. 1920-1925.
Value: $20-$25.

Plate 267.

Maple sugar candy mold
Hand-carved cat, possibly English, c. early 20th century.
Value: $55-$60.

Plate 266.

Tool for winding clothes line
Pine, remnants of red paint, c. early 20th century.
Value: $12-$15.

Plate 268.

Wire fly dome and maple chopping board
Both factory-made, domes found in many sizes, c. 1900.
Value: dome - $16-$18   chopping board - $18-$20.

Plate 269.

Rolling pin
Maple, factory-made, c. 1900-1920.
Value: $12-$14.

Plate 270.

Rolling pin
Maple, factory-made, c. 1880-1890.
Value: $20-$24.

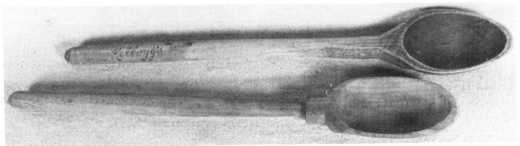

Plate 271.

Kitchen spoons
Maple, factory-made, c. 1920-1930.
Value: $4-$6.

Factory-made spoons were manufactured over a long period of time and changed little in design. These spoons are common and may be purchased for a few dollars in most areas. Heavy use in a kitchen can make new woodenware appear old in a few months.

Plate 272.
Wooden spoon
Maple, hand-carved, refinished, c. 1880-1900.
Value: $15-$17.

Plate 273.
Wooden scoop
Maple, hand-carved, "as found" condition, c. 1860.
Value: $45-$50.

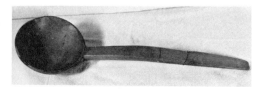

Plate 274.
Wooden spoon or ladle
Maple, hand-carved, refinished, c. 1860
Value: $35-$40.

Plate 275.
Wooden spoon or ladle
Maple, hand-carved, c. 1860.
Value: $35-$40.

Plate 276.
Pestle and small spoon
Maple, hand-carved spoon possibly European, c. 1850.
Value: pestle - $14-$16 spoon - $14-$16.

It is essential that the collector of woodenware be aware of the imported pieces that are being sold. Some of it appears to be very early and offered at bargain prices.

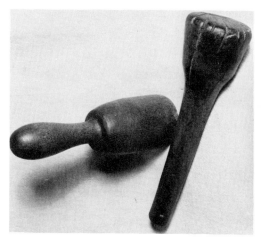

Plate 277.
Early pestles
Interesting comparison between the lathe-turned and the hand-carved, c. 1850-1860.
Value: $14-$16.

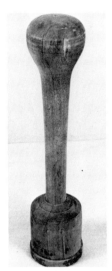

Plate 278.
Pestle and meat pounder
Factory-made, maple, found in New York state, c. 1870.
Value: $20-$22.

Plate 279.

Wooden spoon or ladle
Maple, factory-made, c. 1880.
Value: $18-$22.

Plate 280.

Mirror
4″ x 4″, early glass, maple frame, c. 1830.
Value: $35-$45.

Plate 281.
Foot stool
Pine, half-moon legs, mortised construction, early paint, c. 1840.
Value: $40-$55.

Make a special note to study the construction technique used to fasten the top of the stool to the legs. This is an excellent example of the mortise-and-tenon.

Plate 282.

Foot stool
Walnut, refinished, found in Amana, Iowa, c. 1870.
Value: $50-$60.

Plate 283.

Green bean slicer (back)
Pine, green paint, tin, from Michigan, c. early 20th
century.
Value: $40-$45.

Plate 285.

Lap desk
Walnut, compartmentalized, original condition,
c. 1840-1845.
Value: $75-$85.

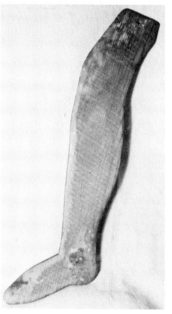

Plate 286.

Sock stretcher
Pine, hand-carved, c. 1900.
Value: $15-$16.

Plate 284.

Green bean slicer (front)

Plate 287.

Egg Box
c. 1930.
Value: $45-$55.

Plate 289.

Grain shovel
Worn red paint, maple, early repair to crack at base of scoop, c. 1860-1870.
Value: $125-$135.

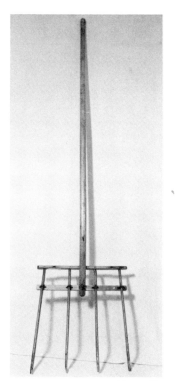

Plate 288.

Hay fork
Maple, refinished, factory-made, c. 1890.
C. 1890.
Value: $75-$95.

Plate 290.

Tin cookie cutter
French, from commercial bakery, 20″ high, c. early 20th century.
Value: $110-$120.
                    (McKnight collection)

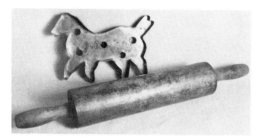

Plate 291.
Tin cookie cutter and tin rolling pin
Maple handles on rolling pin, c. late 19th century.
Value: cookie cutter - $15-$16, rolling pin - $30-$40.

Tin kitchen utensils and cookie cutters are still relatively inexpensive. There is no question that in the near future tin items will appreciate significantly in demand and price. The rolling pin originally was sold with a rectangular tin sheet for rolling dough. The sheet was designed to hang on the wall and had a tray at its base for the rolling pin. If the set were together, the value of the pin and tray would be $65-$75.

Plate 293.
Cookie cutter
Tin, later form, c. early 20th century.
Value: $4-$5.

Plate 292.
Cookie cutters
Tin, strap handles on back, found in eastern Indiana, c. 1870-1900.
Value: man - $20-$30 woman - $20-$30.

Plate 294.
Measure
Tin, probably one of a set of 3-6, c. 1860.
Value: $12-$14.

Plate 295.
Strainer
Tin, probably made and sold by a traveling tinsmith,
c. 1860-1870.
Value: $18-$22.

Plate 297.
Double foot stove
Maple frame, pierced tin top and sides, bail handle,
c. 1830.
Value: $175-$200.

This foot stove contains two small tin buckets for hot coals. Double stoves are much less common than the smaller foot stoves. A conventional foot stove should sell for $75-$85, depending upon its condition.

Plate 296.
Tin container
Small ring handle, c. 1900.
Value: $8-$10.

Plate 298.
Tin pastry cutter and tin raisin container.
c. late 19th century - cutter, c. 1915-1925 - container.
Value: $18-$22 cutter $22-$25 container

Plate 301.

Chopping knife
Earlier form, iron blade, maple handle, c. 1850.
Value: $28-$30.

Plate 299.
Chopping knife and dough scraper
Maple handle and steel blade, wrought iron dough
scraper, c. 1900 - chopping knife, c. 1840 - dough
scraper.
Value: chopping knife - $20-$25, dough scraper -
$14-$16.

Dough scrapers were used to recapture
bits of dough stuck to the bottoms of bowls
or table tops.

Plate 302.
Chopping knife
c. 1880.
Value: $24-$26.

Plate 300.
Chopping knife
c. 1880-1900.
Value: $18-$22.

Plate 303.
Late chopping knife
Maple handle, steel blade, c. 1920.
Value: $18-$22.

Plate 304.

Enterprise coffee grinder
#5 model, original paint and stenciling, early replacement drawer, c. late 19th century.
Value: $225-$240.

Plate 305.

Bell corn grinder
Original black and red paint, c. 1890.
Value: $40-$50.

It is not uncommon for collectors to hear their hearts pounding when they happen upon a wheeled grinder in old paint with a $30 price tag. Unfortunately, the bargain turns out to be a grinder used to grind corn rather than coffee.

Plate 306.

Cannister coffee grinder or mill
Made for hanging on wall, used in the home, c. 1890-1910.
Value: $50-$60.

The early mail order houses sold thousands of these grinders to turn-of-the-century coffee drinkers.

Plate 307.

Tin coffee grinder or mill
c. 1860-1870.
Value: $65-$75.

Plate 308.

Fly dome
Wire, maple, "knob" handle, c. 1880.
Value: $20-$24.

Flies were a major irritant in late 19th century kitchens. Fly domes were found in a variety of sizes and were placed over plates of baked goods or food to keep the flies away. The smaller domes are less commonly found than the larger ones.

Plate 310.

Fresh Eggs sign
Black letters on white background, tin, c. early 20th century.
Value: $30-$35.

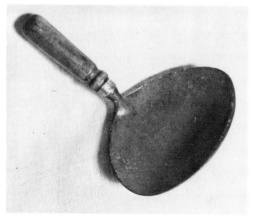

Plate 309.

Iron ladle
Maple handle, early factory-made, c. 1860-1870.
Value: $20-$25.

Plate 311.

Apple butter kettle
Copper, iron bail handle, dovetailed side and bottom, 36" d., c. 1870-1880.
Value: $250-$275.

In the 1960's, a trip into the apple country of southern Illinois could net at least one kettle in every antiques shop.

The kettles were heavily covered with carbon and required dedication or a professional to clean. The kettles have almost vanished at this point to the sides of fireplaces throughout the middle west.

Plate 312.
Iron kettle
"Goose neck" spout, bail handle, New York state, c. 1840.
Value: $85-$100.

Plate 314.
Peel
Iron, hand forged, used to remove bread from a bake oven, c. 1820-1830.
Value: $65-$70.

Plate 313.
Sugar nippers
Hand forged, designed for table use, c. 1780-1800.
Value: $75-$85.

Sugar nippers were used to cut the cones of sugar that were in use during the colonial period. This example was used at the table and passed from diner to diner as the need arose.

Plate 315.
Porringer
Iron, cast in an early mold, c. 1800.
Value: $75-$80.

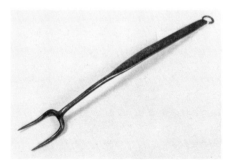

Plate 316.
Toasting fork
Hand forged iron, c. early 19th century.
Value: $50-$55.

Plate 317.

Toasting fork
Hand forged iron, c. early 19th century.
Value: $60-$65.

Plate 318.

Ladle
"Rat tail" hanging hook, c. 1840.
Value: $35-$45.

Plate 319.

Iron toaster
Rotating toaster, 3 legs, hand forged, c. 1830.
Value: $150-$175.

Plate 320.

Cast iron trivet
c. 1870.
Value: $18-$22.

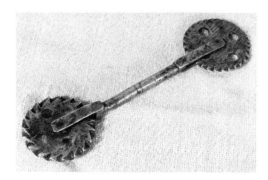

Plate 321.

Pie crimper
c. 1830-1840.
Value: $50-$55.

Plate 322.

Tailor's scissors
c. 1880.
Value: $16-$18.

Plate 323.

Scales
c. late 19th century.
Value: $30-$35.

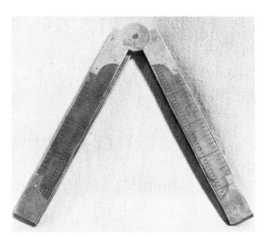

Plate 324.

Folding ruler
Brass and maple, c. 1880.
Value: $18-$22

Plate 326.

Folding ruler
Brass and maple, c. 1880.
Value: $18-$22.

Plate 327.

Wire trivet
c. late 19th century.
Value: $15-$19.

Plate 328.

Vaporizer
Tin, early one for home use, c. 1890-1900.
Value: $30-$35.

Plate 325.

Folding ruler
Brass and maple, c. 1880.
Value: $18-$22.

The screw cap was removed and water was placed in the upper portion of the vaporizer. In the open area below, a small candle provided enough heat to produce a minimal amount of steam.

Plate 329.

Tea and coffee cannisters
Unmarked, stenciled decoration, probably given as
a premium, c. 1880-1900.
Value: $40-$50.

Plate 331.

Tobacco tin
Central Union Cut Plug, "lunchbox"-type, tin, c.
1885.
Value: $40-$60.

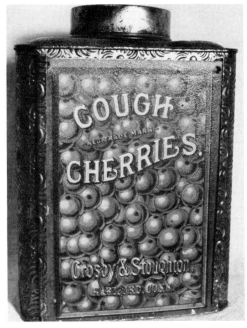

Plate 330.

Cough cherries container
For store use, slide-out label allowed other items
to be stored in the same container with a new label,
c. 1890.
Value: $75-$85.

Plate 332.

Peanut butter tin
Bail handle, c. 1920.
Value: $25-$35.

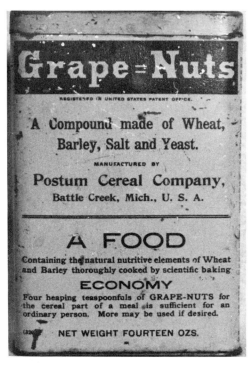

Variety of home remedy bottles
c. late 1800's-early 1900's.
Values: $5-$25.

Plate 335.

Plate 333.

Cereal tin
"Grape Nuts," black and yellow decoration, c. 1900.
Value: $65-$85.

In the late 1960's, a large number of Oceanic Cut Plug and Dan Patch Cut Plug tins were found in a Detroit warehouse and offered by an Ohio dealer in the Antique Trader. The tins were priced at less than $10 and were in mint condition.

Plate 334.

Candy container
"Dixie Queen" stick candy, c. 1930.
Value: $14-$16.

Plate 336.

Tobacco and food tins
c. late 1800's-early 1900's.
Values: $5-$45.

Plate 337.

Flour container
c. 1880.
Value: $50-$60.

Plate 338.

Wafer tin
c. 1940.
Value: $5-$7.

Plate 339.

Mustard plaster tin
c. 1930.
Value: $5-$7.

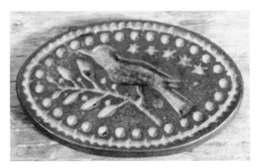

Plate 340.

Oval cake mold
Cast iron, New York state, c. 1820-1830.
Value: $70-$75.

Plate 341.

"Turk's Turbin" cake mold
Cast iron, New York state, c. 1870.
Value: $35-$45.

Plate 342.

Fire bucket
"Sand for Fire Only" - stenciled, c. 1880.
Value: $50-$60.

Plate 344.

Iron pot
Bail handle, 3 iron legs, c. 1890.
Value: $30-$35.

Plate 343.

Fry pan
Cast iron, found in W. Virginia, c. early 20th century.
Value: $18-$22.

Plate 345.

Iron pot
Bail handle, 3 raised legs, possibly European, c. 1850.
Value: $45-$55.

Plate 348.

Pewter ladle with turned wood handle
c. 1820.
Value: $100-$115.

Plate 346.
Copper warming pan
Incised decoration on lid, found in Pennsylvania,
c. 1830.
Value: $200-$225.

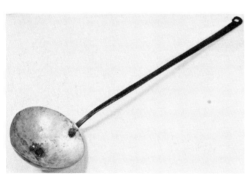

Plate 347.
Iron and brass ladle
c. 1830.
Value: $65-$75.

Plate 349.
Brass skimmer
Iron handle, copper nails, Pennsylvania, c. 1840.
Value: $100-$110.

Plate 350.

Brass skimmer with iron handle
c. 1820
Value: $100-$110.

Plate 352.

Copper ladle with iron handle
Probably European, c. 19th century.
Value: $35-$40.

This is another example of an imported kitchen utensil that is sold as American-made. It is also crudely constructed when it is compared with American craftsmanship.

Plate 351.

Brass ladle with iron handle
Probably European, copper patches, c. 19th century.
Value: $55-$60.

Compare the workmanship of this ladle and the example in Plate 349 with the other skimmers and ladles. The workmanship is obviously inferior to the American utensils.

Plate 353.

Brass skimmer with iron handle
c. 1830.
Value: $70-$75.

Plate 354.

Brass kitchen scoop
c. 1890.
Value: $25-$28.

Plate 357.

Tin candy mold
Made by hammering in a mold, c. 1880.
Value: $20-$22.

Plate 355.

Cottage cheese drainer
Tin, bow handles, New York state, c. 1850-1860.
Value: $55-$65.

Plate 358.

Iron trivet and pewter candlestick
c. 1840.
Value: trivet - $40-$45   candlestick - $60-$65.

Plate 356.

Wall clock
Made in Waterbury, Conn., key wound mechanism,
c. 1880-1890.
Value: $130-$140.

The trivet is similar to many that have been imported in the past decade from Europe. The unmarked candlestick is English and dates from the mid-1800's.

Plate 359.

Tin candleholder
c. 1850.
Value: $40-$45.

Plate 361.

Tin candleholder
Designed to be stuck in a beam or small opening,
c. 1830.
Value: $50-$55.

Plate 362.

Iron candleholder
"Hog-scraper" type, tab to adjust candle height,
c. 1840.
Value: $55-$60.

"Hog-scraper" candlesticks are similar in design to a common midwestern tool that was used to scrape bristles from hogs at butchering time each fall. A hog-scraper has a wooden handle and an iron base.

The rarest "hog-scraper" candlestick has a brass ring around the center of the shaft. A "hog-scraper" with a "wedding ring" on its shaft is worth at least $90-$125.

Plate 360.

Tin candleholder
Finger hold, slide tab to regulate candle height,
c. 1850.
Value: $50-$55.

Plate 363.

Tin candleholder
Saucer base, finger hold, tab to adjust candle height,
c. 1840.
Value: $65-$70.

Plate 365.

Saucer candleholder
Tin, finger hold, c. 1975.
Value: $18-$20.

This is a reproduction that was allowed
to sit in the rain and snow for a winter and
emerged as a century-old rarity. The un-
initiated would stand in line to purchase
a similar piece for $65-$75.

Plate 364.

Pair of Queen Anne candlesticks
Cast brass, English, c. 1750.
Value: $160-$180.

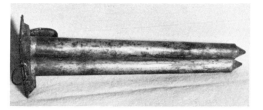

Plate 366.

Tin candlemold
Two-tube, strap handle, hanging ring, c. 1840.
Value: $55-$60.

Plate 367.

Tin candlemold
Strap handle, miniature, for making Christmas tree candles, 12 tubes, c. 1850.
Value: $250-$300.

Plate 369.

Tin candlemold
18-tube, two strap handles, c. 1850.
Value: $85-$95.

Plate 368.

Tin candlemolds
12-tube, hanging 3-tube mold, c. 1850.
Value: 12-tube mold - $70-$75   3-tube mold - $50-$55.

Plate 370.

Tin candlemold
4-tube, hanging, strap handle, c. 1850.
Value: $40-$45.

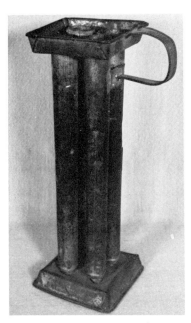

Plate 371.
Tin candlemold
4-tube standing mold, strap handle, c. 1850.
Value: $50-$55.

Plate 373.
Tin candlemold
6-tube, on four splayed legs, c. 1850.
Value: $150-$175.

Plate 372.
Tin candlemold
6-tube standing mold, strap handle, c. 1850.
Value: $55-$60.

Plate 374.
Pierced tin candle lantern
Original early condition, called "Paul Revere" lantern, c. 1840.
Value: $135-$145.

These have been reproduced since the early 1900's, and many early reproductions now carry all the attributes of distinguished old age.

122

Plate 375.

Candle lantern
Tin frame, glass sides, wire guards, factory-made,
c. 1860.
Value: $75-$85.

Compare the designs punched into the tin in Plates 374 and 375. The tin in Plate 375 was stamped rather than hand pierced in a random fashion. Lamps of this type have often lost their oil burner and been replaced with a "make-do" candle socket.

Plate 376.

Wood framed candle lantern
Pine and glass, c. 1840-1850.
Value: $110-$115.

Plate 377.

Iron lamp holder
Hand forged iron, hook for hanging, spike, probably European, c. 1830.
Value: $50-$55.

Plate 378.

Crusie
Hand wrought iron, half-moon decoration, twisted iron hook, c. early 19th century.
Value: $100-$115.

The main difference between a crusie and a betty lamp is the wick support in the betty that allowed the oil or grease to run back into the lamp rather than onto the floor or shoulder of a slumbering early American.

123

Plate 379.

Trammel candle holder
Hand wrought iron, sawtooth ratchet adjustable to
seven heights, c. 1820.
Value: $375-$400.

Plate 381.

Rush holder
Candle socket counterweight, birch base, New
York state, c. 1800-1820.
Value: $285-$325.

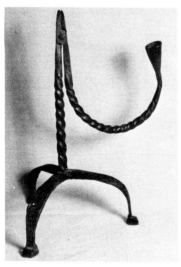

Plate 380.

Rush holder
Candle socket counterweight, twisted iron shaft
for added strength, c. 1800-1820.
Value: $160-$175.

Plate 382.

Kerosene lamp
Tin, strap handle, tin shade, c. 1860.
Value: $125-$135.

Kerosene came into use in the early
1860's and remained the primary lighting
source in the American home until the
early 1900's.

Plate 383.

Watchman's or lens lantern
Bull's-eye lens to magnify amount of light, whale oil light source, c. 1840.
Value: $85-$95.

Plate 385.

Kerosene coach lamp
Used in railroad coaches or cars, tin and glass, stamped decoration, c. 1870.
Value: $75-$80.

Plate 384.

Miner's cap lamp
Coffee pot-shaped font, wick, tin reflector, hinged cover, c. 1900.
Value: $25-$30.

This example and the "Sticking Tommy" candlestick often appear to be much earlier than they are. Both may be found in Sears Roebuck catalogues of the early 1900's.

Plate 386.

Railroad lantern
Tin and glass, tin handle, whale oil light source, c. 1850.
Value: $85-$95.

Plate 387.
Railway lantern
Wire guard, tin and glass, camphene light source, c. 1850.
Value: $85-$95.

Plate 388.
Match holder
Cast iron, designed to be hung on a wall, c. 1870.
Value: $30-$35.

Plate 389.
Branding iron
Forged iron, from the American southwest, c. 1860-1870.
Value: $18-$25.

The wooden handle of this branding iron has been removed and the socket used as a candle holder.

Plate 390.
Tin lamps
c. 1900-1920.
Value: $12-$20.

These imported tin lamps are deceiving, because they appear to be very early. They have been imported by the thousands and are relatively inexpensive in most shops.

Plate 391.

Coach or carriage light
Glass and brass, polished reflector, c. 1880.
Value: $70-$75.

Plate 392.

Candle holders
Designed to hang on the wall, lathe-turned maple,
c. 1880-1890.
Value: $55-$60.

Preliminary Quiz IV

1. Which of the lists below is correct chronologically in the development of lighting?
   a. rush light, kerosene, whale oil
   b. candlemold, kerosene, whale oil
   c. whale oil, candle, rush light
   d. rush light, whale oil, kerosene

2. Which of the butter mold or print designs below are you **least** likely to find?
   a. geometric pattern
   b. eagle
   c. swan
   d. wheat

3. True   False   Burl bowls were mass-produced in large quantities in the late 1800's and offered in mail-order catalogs.

Answers may be found on page 164.

Prices of 101 Hearth and Kitchen Antiques Sold at Garth's in 1977

1. Tole cannister, black ground, colorful decoration of fruit and foliage, 8½" h. - $120
2. Tin cookie cutter, bird, 4¼" l. - $11
3. Tin cookie cutter, rooster, 3¾" w. - $16
4. Wooden-staved pail, grained exterior, red metal band, 11" d. - $37.50
5. Tin rolling pin with wooden handles, 17" l. - $45
6. Kraut chopper with wooden handle, 8" w. - $20
7. Oval birdseye maple bowl, hand tool marks, 22½" l. - $165
8. Burl bowl, 13½" d. - $270
9. Burl butter scoop, 8" l. - $205
10. Wrought iron pastry cutter with brass wheel, "T. Loose", 8¼" l. - $20
11. Small tin cup, embossed exterior has worn green japanning - $4
12. Curly maple rolling pin, 18½" l. - $42.50
13. Small spun brass pail, 8¼" d. x 5" h. - $35
14. Wrought iron kraut chopper with wooden handle, base is 4" wide - $15
15. Walnut fire board, 3 raised panels, 49" x 35¾" - $110
16. Wrought-iron scissors wick trimmer, 6¼" h. - $17.50
17. Spun brass kettle with iron stationary handle, 13¼" d. x 13" h. - $35
18. Tin pencil case, worn red paint, with yellow stenciling, "A Present", 7½" l. - $17.50
19. Spun brass pail with brass ring handles, 13¾" d. x 8" h. - $35
20. Weighted tin candlestick cone base with crimped ring as base and one as drip pan, handle, 4¾" d. x 5" - $130
21. Small heavy sheet copper pitcher, 3½" h. - $17.50
22. Small wrought-iron fireplace shovel, damaged blade, 24" l. - $2.
23. Iron ice tongs, spring added to handles so points will hold paper towels - $10
24. Cast-iron frog door stop, no paint, 3" h. - $25
25. Cast-iron waffle iron with wrought iron handles, 28" l. - $85
26. Wrought-iron peel, heart scroll handle, 46" l. - $125
27. Wrought-iron saw tooth trammel, 30" h. - $45
28. Three iron fluting irons - $7.50
29. Dog, bird, heart cookie cutters - $15
30. Wooden springerle rolling pin, 13" h. - $30
31. Two iron scissors wick trimmers, 6" l. - $12.50
32. Tin candle lantern, ring handle, decorative star and triangle vents in top, 15" h. - $50
33. Miniature wrought-iron flat iron, 4¼" l. x 2¼" h. - $22.50
34. 12-tube tin candlemold, one handle missing, repair needed - $15
35. Small tin nutmeg grater, 5" l. and a 12-tube tin candlemold - $22
36. Cast-iron gypsy kettle with wrought iron handle, 12" d. x 7½" h. - $37.50
37. Cast-iron skillet on 3 feet, "11" on handle, 11" d. x 5¼" h. - $37.50
38. Brass scissor wick trimmers, 6" l. - $22.50
39. Oval tin dish pan with iron handles, 21" x 17" x 5¼" h. - $17.50
40. Cast-iron gypsy kettle, wrought iron handle, 14" d. x 10" h. - $35
41. Tailor's iron with removable wooden handle, 8" l. - $15
42. Cast-iron flat iron, 6¼" l. - $4
43. Turned wooden bowl, 17½" d. - $20
44. Pair of cast-iron G. Washington andirons, cast initials "ESC DB VA", 15" h. - $200
45. 2 iron hog scraper candlesticks, one is missing pushup, one is missing hanger, 7" and 8" h. - $30
46. Wrought-iron fork, 16¾" l. - $20
47. Wrought-iron and brass strainer, 18" l. - $50
48. Olive green blown globular bottle, 12½" h. - $80
49. Round bentwood box, painted exterior, 5¾" d. - $8
50. Amber fruit jar, "Trade Mark, Lightning" lid with wire fastener, 8" h. - $27.50
51. Small oval bentwood box, 6" l. - $45
52. Small oval bentwood box, 4" l. - $32.50
53. Brass hog scraper candlestick, pushup and lip hanger, 5¼" h. - $67.50
54. 2 pewter spoons, teaspoon and rattail tablespoon - $6
55. Aqua fruit jar, "Mason Fruit Jar" zinc lid, 8¾" h. - $5
56. Cobalt blue blown bottle, probably a nursing bottle, 7¼" l. - $95
57. Amber fruit jar, "Trade Mark, Lightning", 10¼" h., glass lid and wire fastener - $55
58. Amber fruit jar, "Globe", glass lid and fastener - $40
59. Stone wooden sugar bucket, 9½" d., damage to lid and one band - $30
60. Copper wash boiler, turned wooden handles, 27½" l. - $35
61. Bell metal school bell, turned wooden handle, 9" h. - $20
62. Curly maple cutting board, 14" x 24½" - $102.50
63. Fabric stamp, 1¾" x 3½" x 6" - $7

64. Iron sewing bird with tiny red pincushion on bird's back, 5" h. - $77.50
65. Iron pincushion, clamps to table top, thumb screw has heart, 6¼" l. - $70
66. Tin cookie cutter, eagle, 3¼" h. - $15
67. Tin cookie cutter, bird - $6
68. Tin cookie cutter, rooster - $16
69. Tin cookie cutter, boot, 3¾" h. - $22
70. Wooden scoop, one piece of wood, 13½" l. - $100
71. Pine and maple sugar mold, 81 scalloped cut-outs, 12" x 39" - $205
72. Brass betty lamp, wrought iron hanger, 4½" l. - $85
73. Iron tasting spoon, 8¼" l. - $35
74. Tasting spoon, brass bowl, iron handle, 10" l. - $80
75. Hanging wooden towel rack, shows some age, 24" w. x 10" d. x 26½" h. - $80
76. Turned wooden covered jar, age crack in base held by staples and wire band, 11" d. x 8" h. - $35
77. Goffering iron and holder, signed base, 15" l. - $50
78. Tin baking mold in the shape of a lamb 13¼" l. - $65
79. Tin fish baking mold, 12¾" l. - $25
80. Deep burl bowl, 14" d. x 6½" h. - $475
81. Tin foot warmer, wire handle, 7¾" x 8½" x 3¾" h. - $85
82. Small burl bowl, 6" d. - 2¼" h. - $475
83. Tin cookie cutter, woman with crimped skirt, 3" h. - $22.50

84. Tin cookie cutter, seated dog, 3¼" h. - $16
85. Tin cookie cutter, man in the moon, 4½" h. - $230
86. Tin cookie cutter, hand and heart, 3¾" h. - $132.50
87. Burl bowl, flared sides with wide rim, age crack in rim, 17" d. - $300
88. Pair of tin candle sconces, crimped circle top, 13" h. - $165
89. Wrought-iron dough scraper, 5" l. - $12.50
90. Punched tin Paul Revere lantern, slightly battered, 13¼" h. - $70
91. American pewter coffee pot, "Boardman and Co. New York" - $305
92. Pair of pewter candlesticks, 9¾" h. - $160
93. Pewter plate, nicely formed rim, 10¼" d. - $55
94. American pewter teapot, "Putnam", battered base, 8½" h. - $170
95. American pewter charger, two eagle touch marks, "Boardman Warranted", 13½" d. - $350
96. Tin whale oil lamp, saucer base, tapered stem with handle, single spout burner, 4¾" d. x 8" h. - $125
97. Primitively carved stone mortar and pestle, American Indian origin, 7" d. - $50
98. Pair of pewter whale oil lamps, double spout burners, 8" h. - $210
99. Pewter and tin funnel, slightly battered, 4½" l. - $20
100. Brass Queen Anne candlestick, 7" h. - $65
101. Round wooden sheaf of wheat, butter print, long handle, 3½" d. x 6½" l.

7. Potpourri

It is difficult to categorize many types of country antiques into specific areas. Our hope is that you have taken the time to study the pictures and prices and have gained some information about early things. Items in this section range from samplers to trade signs to toys.

Trade Signs

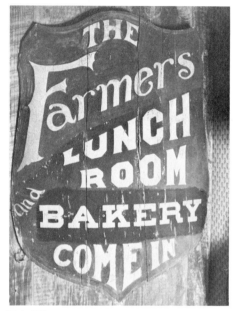

Plate 393.

Restaurant sign
Found in New Hampshire, green with white lettering, pine, c. 1870-1890.
Value: $250-$275.

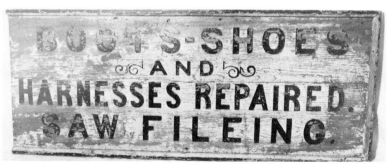

Plate 394.

A problem with any trade sign used outdoors is weathering damage. This sign borders on the realm of being too rough. It measures 42" x 22".

Repairman's sign
Pine, white with black lettering, found in southern Illinois, c. 1920-1930.
Value: $95-$110.

Plate 395.

Trade sign
Pine, 13″ x 18″, found in central Illinois, blue with white lettering, c. 1900-1910.
Value: $85-$110.

This is a fairly standard exterior sign. It is not unusual nor exceedingly well executed.

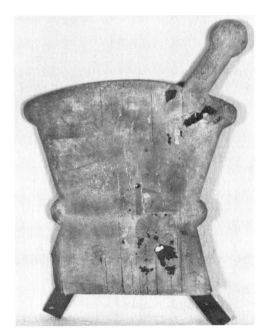

Plate 396.

Pharmacy sign
Pine, gold leaf over green paint, 20″ x 14″, c. 1870.
Value: $100-$115.

Plate 397.

In 1870, an individual did not have to be able to read to know that the store from which this sign hung sold laxatives and liniment.

Restaurant sign
Found in northern Wisconsin, tin in pine frame, c. 1930.
Value: $120-$125.

Plate 400.

Shoe store sign
Pine, yellow with black lettering, interior sign, c. 1930-1940.
Value: $40-$50.

Plate 398.

Paint sampler
Maple, various colors, decal lettering, interior sign, c. 1880-1900.
Value: $150-$175.

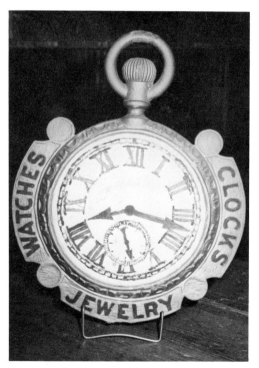

Plate 399.

Tavern sign
English, interior sign, c. 1900.
Value: $175-$190.

Plate 401.

Jewelry sign
Cast zinc, gold, white, black lettering, exterior sign.
Hands usually set at 8:16 to 8:20, c. 1880.
Value: $135-$145.

Plate 402.

Jewelry sign
Cast zinc, black and white, c. 1880.
Value: $100-$115.

Plate 404.

Physician's sign
From Fairbury, Ill., tin, black with gold lettering, exterior sign, c. 1875.
Value: $50-$70.

Plate 405.

Tin sign
New England, black with white lettering, interior sign, c. 1900.
Value: $45-$55.

Plate 403.

Barber shop sign
From Baltimore hotel, copper, brass letters, c. 1900.
Value: $300-$325.

Plate 406.

Town line sign
Cast aluminum, grey with black lettering, c. 1940.
Value: $30-$40.

Odds and Ends

Plate 407.

Windmill weight
Cast-iron cow, base added, found in Nebraska, c. 1900.
Value: $85-$100.

Plate 409.

Cast-iron display boot from shoe store
Gold boot, red buttons, black heel, c. 1880-1890.
Value: $60-$65.

Plate 408.

Tin roof ornament
Hand-made, red paint, common on mid-Victorian homes, c. 1880-1890.
Value: $60-$65.

Plate 410.

Cast-iron hitching horse
New horses are being cast from old molds and allowed to weather, c. 1970.
Value: $20-$25.   old example: $125-$135

Plate 411.

Whirligig
Carved pine, Union soldier, new base, c. 1870-1900.
Value: $200-$215.

Plate 412.

Carved grasshopper
Pine, worn paint, tool marks, possibly a trade sign, c. 1870.
Value: $200-$215.

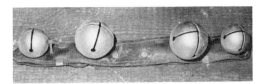

Plate 413.

Harness bells
Nickel-plated brass bells - leather strap, c. 1890-1900.
Value: $50-$60.

Plate 414.

Cast sundial
c. 1900.
Value: $50-$55.

Plate 415.

Tin mouse trap
c. 1860.
Value: $15-$18.

Plate 416.
Carved straight razor
Tin blade, maple handle, found in New York state, c. 1870.
Value: $35-$45.

Plate 418.
Tin tobacco mold
Used to imprint design on tobacco plugs, North Carolina, c. 1910.
Value: $15-$18.

Plate 417.
Printed birth certificate
Pennsylvania, hand water-colored, c. 1845.
Value: $60-$65.

Plate 419.
Copper stencil
Used in Crystal Spring Creamery, c. 1880.
Value: $12-$14.

Plate 420.

Checker board
Pine, red, black and white paint, c. 1900-1910.
Value: $50-$60.

Plate 422.

Roasted coffee store container
c. 1880.
Value: $85-$95.

Plate 421.

Store pepper container
Holds 100 pounds, maple top, paper sides, c. 1880.
Value: $60-$65.

Plate 423.

Seed box (interior)
c. 1900.
Value: $80-$90.

Plate 424.

Seed box (exterior)

Plate 425.

Doll cradle
Walnut, heart cut-out, early red paint, c. 1830.
Value: $85-$100.

Wood cannon
Gold gun, blue carriage, red trim, c. 1880.
Value: $125-$135.

Plate 426.

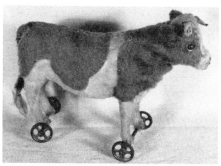

Plate 427.

Toy cow
Cast-iron wheels, brown and white fur, c. 1900.
Value: $85-$100.

Plate 430.

Cast-iron cat bank, block box, ball
c. 1900-1915.
Values: iron cat - $25-$28   block box - $6-$8,
ball - $4-$6

Plate 428.

Child's pull-toy horse
c. 1900.
Value: $55-$60.

Plate 431

Hotpoint child's stove
c. 1930-1940.
Value: $45-$55.

Plate 429.

Cast-iron railroad car
c. 1920.
Value: $14-$18.

Plate 432.

Carved wood toy
c. 1920.
Value: $20-$25.

Textiles

Plate 433.

Framed sampler
Early maple frame, dated 1872, ''Jane Ann Dunn''
Value: $150-$165.

Plate 435.

Sampler
Dated 1832.
Value: $135-$150.

Plate 434.

Sampler
Memorial to Mary Laing, dated 1847.
Value: $150-$165.

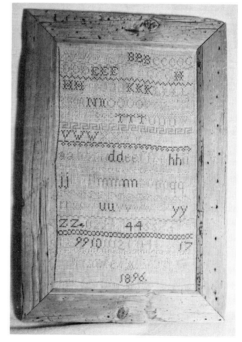

Plate 436.

Sampler
Unsigned, dated 1896, late date for a sampler.
Value: $85-$95.

Plate 437.

Sampler
Roster of family, not dated, c. 1860.
Value: $135-$150.

Quilts and Coverlets

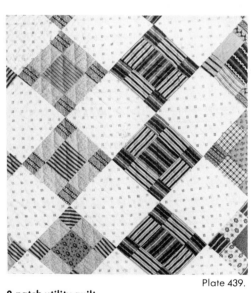

Plate 439.

9-patch utility quilt
Value: $125-$140.

Plate 438.

Two-color quilt
Variation of the "Lady of the Lake" pattern, type of quilt that provides utility with a minimum of quilting.
Value: $125-$140.

This is another example of a utility quilt that does not have significant value. Quilts of this type do have added value if the fabric pieces that make up the quilt are of special interest or quality.

Quilt
Unquilted top - "Star of Le Moyne" pattern.
Value: $45-$55.

Plate 442.

Quilt
A variety of patterns.
Value: $200-$240.

Plate 441.

"Cockscomb Star" quilt.
Trapunto feather wreaths and trailing border.
Value: $450-$500.

The great increase in interest in quilting in the 1970's has given rise to some pricing patterns. Prices on the west coast and the east coast are considerably higher than in the middle west. Many fine examples may still be found in blanket chests and occasional farm sales in Indiana, Missouri, Iowa, Kentucky and Illinois.

This example appears to contain examples of the "Juniper Star" pattern, "Job's Trouble" and "V" blocks at the corners. This is not a common pattern.

Plate 443.

Quilt
9-patch pieced quilt from Fairbury, Illinois.
Value: $125-$150.

"Baskets of Flowers" utility quilt
Pieced variation of the lily or tulip design.
Value: $175-$200.

Overshot coverlet
New York state, c. 1830.
Value: $175-$200.

Jacquard coverlet
Possibly for a child due to small size, produced
from a pattern book, c. 1850.
Value: $100-$120.

Overshot coverlet
New York state, c. 1830.
Value: $175-$200.

Overshot coverlet
New York state, c. 1850.
Value: $140-$150.

Plate 448.

Jacquard coverlet
New York state, c. 1840.
Value: $200-$220.

Plate 449.

Pillow cover
C. 20th century.
Value: $8-$10.

Plate 450.

Preliminary Quiz V

1. True   False   A close look at the front of the clock indicates that it is made of pine.

2. The clock front has been:
   a. veneered
   b. grained
   c. decorated with a sponge dipped in a milk base paint

3. True   False   The painting process used on the clock's glass door is called reverse painting.

Answers may be found on page 164.

Prices of 25 Potpourri Antiques Sold at Garth's in 1977

1. Blue, white and olive brown chintz with Washington, flags and eagle, "E. Pluribus Unum" in banner, some deterioration, matted, 19" x 28" - $175
2. Fraktur certificate, hand drawn and colored, vining tulips encircle text recording birth of Rabel Haas in 1837, Berks county, Pa., old mahogany on pine frame, 10½" x 12½" - $300
3. Carved wooden ram, 5½" h. - $105
4. Two cast iron frogs, 5" l. - $25
5. Primitively carved wooden ox with copper harness, 7½" l. - $40
6. Wooden hobby horse, base is missing, worn white paint, has harness and remains of tail, 32½" l. - $115
7. Early smoothing board, fine relief carving with initials "A.L." and date "1711", 4¾" w. x 26" l. - $290
8. Jointed wooden doll, primitively constructed with painted head, no clothes, 11½" h.
9. One-piece, single-weave jacquard coverlet, white, blue, red and pale green, has wear, 68" x 84" - $50
10. Pieced quilt, blazing sun pattern in red calico and white, signed "Plummer" on corner tag, Ohio, c. 1865, 94" sq. - $200
11. Tin campaign torch, wooden handle is cut out in the shape of a long rifle, 66" l. - $90
12. Carved wooden shorebird with inset long wooden beak, beautiful condition, 20th century, 12½" h. - $175
13. Cast white-metal chocolate mold, rabbits, 4½" x 10¼" - $17.50
14. Mirror in heavy walnut on pine frame, 17" x 23" - $20
15. Pair of composition elephants with grey flocking, 6" l. and 2½" h. - $5
16. Small copper bleeding pan, handle is soldered, 3" d. - $12.50
17. Cast-iron checker bank, one leg is repaired, old worn red and black paint, 4¾" h. - $10
18. Child's pieced quilt, Amish with geometric pattern of rich dark colors, new condition, 38" sq. - $75
19. Sampler on home spun, vining floral border with alphabets and verse and house at bottom, unsigned, unframed, 16" x 16" - $40
20. Cast-iron pig, worn white and black paint, 2¼" h. - $40
21. Sheet iron cut-out Indian, very stylish, age is difficult to determine, 16½" h. - $30
22. Cast-brass bust of Lincoln, mounted on cloth-covered board and framed in flame grain mahogany frame, 14" x 17" - $35
23. Sheet metal horse weathervane on iron standard, bullet holes and old aluminum paint, 27" w. x 55" h. overall - $85
24. Woven split wood doll cradle, red and natural, 7½" l. - $5
25. Mirror with leveled, flame-grained mahogany frame, gilt inside moulding, 17½" x 23½" - $22.50

8. Shaker Antiques

On February 26, 1736, Ann Lee was born in Manchester, England. In September, 1758, Ann Lee joined a religious group called the "Shaking Quakers." After a lengthy period of religious persecution and personal tragedy, Lee and eight followers arrived in New York on August 6, 1774. Between 1774 and her death at the age of 48 in 1784, Lee traveled throughout the eastern states gathering converts to a new faith. From Lee's work emerged 19 Shaker communities ranging from Maine to Kentucky that peaked with a membership of about 6,000 members by the 1860's.

The Shakers' rigid lifestyle was especially felt in the furnishings of their living quarters. Beds were to be painted green, blankets were blue and white (stripes and checks were prohibited), one rocking chair was permitted in each room, and mirrors were limited to no more than 18" in width.

In 1868, the Shakers were selling their rocking chairs (sizes 0 to 7) wholesale to dealers in a variety of towns. The only furniture the Shakers ever sold to the "world," which included everyone who was not a Shaker, were rocking chairs and a variety of foot stools. A multitude of other small items were sold to the "world" at shops in the communities. These products include baskets, sewing utensils, boxes and brushes.

In recent years, there has been an increase in the awareness of Shaker craftsmanship. The furniture usually can be easily recognized and documented. Baskets and tinware create a significant problem, because they are seldom signed and are often similar in design to products made by others.

Shaker Chronology

1758 — Ann Lee joins the "Shaking Quakers"
1774 — Lee and 8 followers arrive in New York (August 6)
1776 — First permanent settlement developed in Niskeyuna, N.Y.
1784 — Ann Lee dies
1800 — Shakers begin selling herbs and seeds
1850 — Peak membership of 6000 Shakers
1867-68 — Wholesaling chairs to urban retail stores begins
1874 — First chair catalogue issued
1876 — Shakers win medals for design at Philadelphia Exposition
1900-1938 — Communities at Watervliet, N.Y., Harvard, Mass., Enfield, Conn., Alfred, Me., Enfield, N.H., Shirley, Mass., South Union, Ky., Union Village, Ohio, Watervliet, Ohio, Pleasant Hill, Ky, and Whitewater, Ohio close.
1978 — Two communities (Canterbury, N.H., Sabbathday Lake, Maine) with less than a handful of surviving Shakers remaining.

Shaker combs
c. late 19th century
Value: $30-$40.

Plate 451.

Plate 452.

Tin cheese or curd drainer
c. 1870.
Value: $110-$125.

This is very similar in form and function to the woven curd baskets.

Plate 453.

Rug beater
Wire with maple handle, "Levi Shaw, Mt. Lebanon, N.Y.", c. 1880.
Value: $85-$100.
            (J.A. Honegger collection)

Plate 454.

Tin strainer
Attributed to the Harvard, Mass., Shakers, c. 1860.
Value: $40-$45.

Plate 455.

Clay pipes
Attributed to the Mt. Lebanon Shakers, c. 1870.
Value: $18-$20.

Plate 456.

Tin lamp filler can
Used to fill kerosene lamps, c. 1870-1880.
Value: $50-$75.

Plate 459.

Yarn swift
Harvard, Mass., maple, yellow wash or stain, c. 1880.
Value: $145-$155.

Plate 457.

Dust pan and whisk broom
Broom made from broom corn, turned maple handle, c. 1850.
Value: dust pan - $85-$95 broom - $45-$55.

Plate 460.

Clothes hanger, dusting brush
Turned maple handle, type sold in Shaker community shops, c. 1890-1900.
Value: dusting brush - $60-$65 maple hanger - $29-$25.

Plate 458.

Spice chest
New England, 6 drawers, pine and maple, red stain, c. 1850.
Value: $185-$225.

148

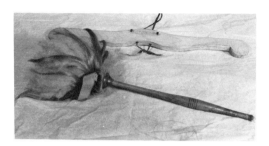

Plate 461.

Maple clothes hanger and dusting brush
Hanger signed "Sisters' side", brush has original ribbons.
c. hanger - 1860   brush - 1890-1900.
Values: hanger - $35-$40, brush - $60-$65.

Plate 464.

Woven horse hair sieve
New England, great color in woven horse hair, c. 1880.
Value: $90-$100.

Plate 462.

Apple butter scoop
Maple, carved from a single piece of wood, c. 1850.
Value: $150-$175.

Plate 465.

Leather sewing kit
Pin cushions in both ends, space for needles and buttons, c. 1910.
Value: $40-$45.

Plate 466.

Pin cushions and leather needle case
The large pin cushion of woven poplar, all three sold in Shaker community shops, c. 1900.
Values: small pin cushion - $12-$14
           large pin cushion - $22-$26
           leather needle case - $10-$12.

Plate 463.

Initials on handle of apple butter scoop

Plate 467.

Mount Lebanon seed box
Lift top, compartmentalized interior, label in excellent condition, c. 1900.
Value: $200-$250.

Mt. Lebanon was known as New Lebanon prior to 1861. A Shaker seed box with a New Lebanon label in good condition would be worth $225-$250. These boxes were distributed to the seed dealers to display on their counters.

Plate 468.

Foot stool
Pine, early green paint, worn top, half-moon cutouts, c. 1840.
Value: $85-$100.

Plate 469.

Foot stool
Replaced tapes, refinished, c. 1880.
Value: $50-$75

Plate 470.

Shaker #3 rocking chair
Replaced tapes, original finish, Mt. Lebanon, N.Y., c. 1880-1890.
Value: $225-$240.

Plate 471.

Decal used on slat of Shaker #3 rocker

Plate 472.

Shaker #7 rocking chair
Replaced tapes, #7 impressed into rear of top slat,
Mt. Lebanon, N.Y., c. 1880-1890.
Value: $300-$350.

Shaker rocking chairs with the Mt. Lebanon decal are worth $15-$20 more than chairs without it. The replaced tapes generally do not affect the value of the chair. The chairs with the impressed number on the rear of the stop slat and/or a decal were production chairs made for the "world", and not for use in the Shaker communities.

Plate 473.

Rocking chair
Replaced tapes, arms with mushroom tenon caps,
cushion rail, c. 1880.
Value: $375-$425.

The bar or rail above the top slat was used to tie a back cushion on the chair. In 1876, the cushions sold for $4 each, the chairs for $10.

Plate 474.

Arm chair
Replaced tapes, original finish, production chair, c. 1880.
Value: $300-$350.

New tapes in the original Shaker designs may be purchased at many of the Shaker restorations.

Plate 475.

Shaker arm chair
Original splint seat, original finish, not a production chair, c. 1830-1840.
Value: $275-$300.

Plate 477.

Shaker dry sink
c. 1840.
Value: $1,100-$1,200.

Plate 476.

Shaker drop front desk
Pine, Enfield, Conn., original finish, c. 1850.
Value: $900-$1,100.

Plate 478.

Berry bucket or pail
Bail handle, yellow exterior, white interior, staved
construction, c. late 19th century.
Value: $85-$95.

The bottom of the pail is signed "E.H.
No. 10." The iron diamond-shaped braces
on the sides of the pail are typical of Shaker
construction in staved buckets or pails.

Plate 479.

Berry bucket or pail
Staved construction, iron bands, "diamond" braces,
5" d., c. late 19th century.
Value: $75-$85.

Plate 481.

Field bucket
Maple handle, blue paint, original condition, staved
construction, leather spout, c. 1860.
Value: $275-$300.

Plate 480.

Berry bucket or pail
Staved construction, iron bands, "diamond" braces,
deep red paint, c. late 19th century.
Value: $75-$85.

Plate 482.

Swing handle storage box
Lid, soft red paint, original condition, c. 1870.
Value: $125-$135.

Plate 483.

Swing handle box
Copper nails, original unpainted finish, "Hancock, Mass." impressed in bottom, c. 1900.
Value: $75-$95.

Plate 485.

Bucket
Original condition, "diamond" braces, staved construction, unpainted, c. 1900.
Value: $55-$60.

Plate 484.

Cheese box
Yellow paint, button hoop construction, impressed "Harvard", c. 1860.
Value: $120-$130.

Plate 486.

Carrier
Yellow "wash," finger lap construction, maple sides, pine bottom, copper nails, c. 1870.
Value: $300-$350.

Plate 487.

Carrier
Finger lap construction, four "fingers", remnants of red stain, c. 1870.
Value: $300-$350.

Plate 488.

Oval box
Light green paint, four "fingers", copper nails, c. second half of 19th century.
Value: $200-$240.

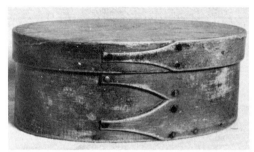

Plate 489.

Back side of Shaker oval box
Yellow paint, "P.C." in red, five fingers, c. 1830.
Value: $350-$400.

Plate 490.

Oval box
Finger lap construction, blue paint, copper nails, c. second half of 19th century.
Value: $225-$250.

In the bottom of the lid of this oval box is the following history:

"Polly Congleton gave this box to Eldress Pauline Bryant when she died Aug. 3, 1833"

In another person's handwriting is the following:

"Given me Aug. 1886 by Eldress Pauline Bryant on her death bed."

Pleasant Hill Kentucky

Plate 491.

Oval box
Finger lap construction, bittersweet colored paint, four "fingers", c. second half of 19th century.
Value: $300-$350.

Oval box

Plate 492.

Finger lap construction, copper nails, two "fingers",
5½" x 3", yellow paint, c. second half of 19th
century.
Value: $165-$175.

This box appears to have been made by
the Harvard, Mass., Shakers.

Plate 494.

Oval boxes

Unpainted original condition, finger lap construction,
copper nails, c. second half of 19th century.
Value: $155-$175.

Oval box

Plate 493.

Finger lap construction, copper nails, two fingers,
blue paint, c. second half of 19th century.
Value: $200-$225.

A close look at this box shows part of a
third "finger" hidden under the side of the
lid. This box could legitimately be advertised as a two-or three-finger box.

Painted boxes are more eagerly sought
after by collectors than unpainted boxes.
The bittersweet box in Plate 491 and various
shades of blue boxes are the most uncommon. A potential buyer of a Shaker box
in "original" paint should look carefully
for legitimate signs of wear. The two boxes
in Plate 494 would have their value increased by at least 25% to 30% if they
were painted.

Plate 495.

Oval boxes

Dark green paint, made by Harvard, Mass., Shakers,
c. 1850.
Value: $150-$155 each.

Compare the fingers in these boxes with
the construction techniques of the box in
Plate 492.

Plate 496.
Bonnet of woven poplar with attached neck shade
c. 1890.
Value: $60-$75.

Plate 498.
Bonnet
Woven poplar, c. 1890.
Value: $50-$55.

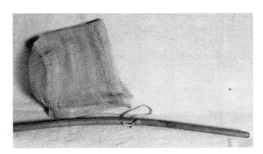

Plate 499.
Bonnet and clothes hanger
Summer-weight bonnet, maple hanger, c. 1850.
Values: bonnet - $55-$60 hanger - $30-$35

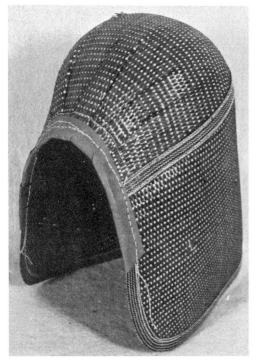

Plate 497.
Bonnet
Woven poplar, size #6, c. 1880-1890.
Value: $50-$55

Plate 500.
The Shaker Manifesto
Printed between 1871-1900, mint original condition,
c. copy dated 1881.
Value: $25-$30.

Plate 501.
Framed Shaker string bean label
Mt. Lebanon, New York, great graphics, c. early 1900's.
Value: $40-$45 (framed)

Plate 502.
Miniature sieve
3″ diameter, original condition, woven hair, c. late 19th century.
Value: $80-$100.

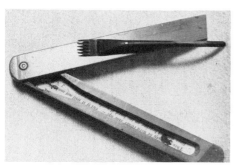

Plate 503.
Musical notation pen
Cherry case, five-pointed pen used to draw staff, designed by Isaac Young, c. mid-19th century.
Value: $350-$375.

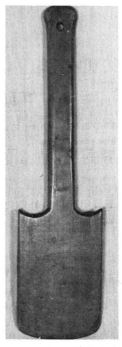

Plate 504.
Wooden kitchen utensil
Maple, hand-made, c. 1860.
Value: $40-$45.

Plate 505.
Clothes scrubber
c. mid-19th century.
Value: $20-$30.

Plate 506.

Wooden scoop
Maple, carved from a single piece of wood, c. late 19th century.
Value: $50-$65.

Plate 508.

Darning egg
Wooden ball revolves in maple case, c. late 19th century-early 20th century.
Value: $35-$40.

Plate 507.

Hand mirror
c. 1860.
Value: $50-$60.

Plate 509.

Pin cushion-spool holder
Turned maple base and stem, made and sold at Sabbathday Lake, Maine, c. 20th century.
Value: $125-$150.

Plate 510.
Sabbathday Lake gum-backed label from pincushion

Plate 512.

Tin churn
Wooden dasher, tin handles, c. 1860.
Value: $200-$250.

Plate 511.
Tin dust pan
c. late 19th century.
Value: $35-$40

Plate 513.
Wooden stirring tool used with tin churn
c. 1860.
Value: $22-$26.

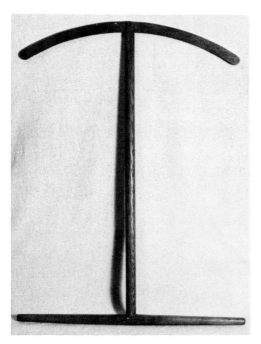

Plate 516.

Brushes
c. late 19th century.
Value: $35-$45 each.

Plate 514.

Cloak hanger
c. late 19th century.
Value: $100-$125.

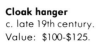

Plate 515.

Brushes and clothes hanger
Turned maple handle, colored velvet, maple hanger,
c. late 19th century.
Values: brushes - $35-$45 each
         hanger - $32-$36.

Plate 517.

Brush
Maple handle, red painted metal rim, c. late 19th
century.
Value: $25-$35.

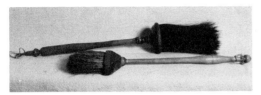

Plate 518.

Brushes
c. late 19th century-early 20th century.
Value: $40-$50.

Plate 519.

Flat broom
Maple handle, iron bands, attributed to the Shakers,
c. 1870.
Value: $130-150.

Plate 520.

Round carrier
Green paint, swing handle, maple sides, pine bottom, attributed to the Shakers, c. 1880.
Value: $75-$85.

Preliminary Quiz VI

1. This Shaker seed box from Mt. Lebanon, New York dates from:
   a. prior to 1862
   b. after 1862

2. True   False   A #9 Shaker rocking chair would be easier to locate than either a #3 or #4.

3. True   False   The most commonly found examples of Shaker furniture made for the "world" were the rocking chairs.

Answers may be found on page 164.

Sabbathday Lake, Maine Auction

June 20, 1972

Shaker antiques have been collected by a growing number of individuals since the publication in the late 1920's of an article by Edward and Faith Andrewson the magazine Antiques. To understand prices today it might be worthwhile to look back at a major Shaker auction in 1972. Many people at the auction realized this probably was one of the last great opportunities to buy documented Shaker antiques from one of the two remaining communities.

1. Dasher butter churn, 20" tall, piggin handle, $500
2. Watervliet, twin size bed, maple, wooden rollers, $475
3. Flour bag, "Shaker mills," New Glouster, $230
4. One "hank" of Shaker-made thread in blue, $27.50
5. Catalog of "fancy" goods - $100
6. Handled laundry basket, signed Sarah Collins, 14"x19"x8" deep, $40
7. Large spinning wheel, $375
8. Seed box with Mt. Lebanon label, $162.50
9. Hancock small swift in yellow paint - $175
10. 9" bottle, aqua, label reading "Shaker Pickles," $162
11. Alfred sewing desk, 12 drawers and pull out slide, butternut and maple, $3,250

Answers to Preliminary Quizzes I-VI

Preliminary Quiz I

1. d
2. b
3. c

Preliminary Quiz II

1. c
2. True
3. c

Preliminary Quiz III

1. d
2. a
3. False

Preliminary Quiz IV

1. d
2. b
3. False

Preliminary Quiz V

1. False
2. a
3. False

Preliminary Quiz VI

1. b
2. False
3. True

Final Examination

After digesting a book of this type, it appears necessary to us that you need an exercise to determine your general knowledge in the field of American country antiques. We have devised the 50 questions below to test your skills of retention, recognition and evaluation.

Read each question carefully and choose the most appropriate response. You can then check your answers for accuracy on pages 176 & 177.

Plate A

1. The 3-gallon crock in Plate A dates from:
   a. prior to 1820
   b. 1820-1850
   c. after 1870

2. The decoration was applied:
   a. with a process called incising
   b. with a brush
   c. with a stencil
   d. none of the above are correct

3. The approximate value of this crock is:
   a. under $20
   b. between $25 and $50
   c. between $75 and $100
   d. more than $100

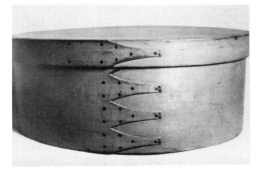

Plate B

4. This box in Plate B was made by the:
   a. Amish
   b. Pennsylvania Dutch
   c. early colonists
   d. none of the above

5. The nails used in the construction of this box are made of:
   a. copper
   b. iron
   c. pewter
   d. brass

6. The approximate value of this box is:
   a. under $20
   b. between $25 and $50
   c. between $75 and $100
   d. more than $100

Plate C

7. The canning jar in Plate C is made of:
   a. red ware
   b. stoneware

8. The primary decoration on the jar was applied:
   a. with a brush
   b. with a stencil
   c. neither of the above

9. T F The wooden lid on the jar was original to the piece.

Plate D

10. T F The spice box in Plate D is constructed of walnut.

11. The spice box dates from:
    a. prior to 1820
    b. between 1840-1860
    c. after 1880

12. The approximate value of the spice box is:
    a. under $25
    b. between $25 and $50
    c. more than $75 but less than $150
    d. more than $175

Plate E

13. The item illustrated in Plate E is:
    a. a cookie mold
    b. a butter print
    c. a butter mold
    d. none of the above

14. Like most pieces of wooden ware, this is made of:
    a. chestnut
    b. pine
    c. poplar
    d. none of the above

15. This example was:
    a. factory-made
    b. hand-carved rather than factory-made

Plate F

16. The 12-tube candle mold in Plate F is made of:
    a. pewter
    b. tin
    c. copper

17. A professional candlemaker was called:
    a. a whitesmith
    b. a chandler
    c. neither of the above

18. The approximate value of the candlemold is:
    a. $10-$25
    b. $30-$45
    c. $55-$85
    d. $140-$165

Plate G

19. The pine bucket bench in Plate G dates from approximately:

   a. the mid-1800's
   b. 1800-1820
   c. 1840-1860
   d. 1870-1880

20. The stretchers are _____ into the legs of the bench.

   a. mortised
   b. dovetailed
   c. neither of the above

21. The value of the bucket bench would be approximately:

   a. under $100
   b. $101-$200
   c. $201-$300
   d. $301-$400

Plate H

22. The material used in the construction of this basket was:

   a. ash splint
   b. rattan
   c. oak splint
   d. none of the above

23. This basket was made:

   a. on a lightship off the coast of Mass.
   b. by Indians in Maine
   c. in the late 18th century in New England
   d. none of the above

24. What other distinctive feature does this basket possess?

   a. uncommonly fine oak splint
   b. open sieve-like bottom
   c. a wooden turned bottom

Plate I

25. This plate is made of:

    a. tin
    b. pewter
    c. cast iron

26. The approximate value of this plate in mint condition is:

    a. $5-$10
    b. $30-$50
    c. $75-$100
    d. $125-$150

27. This plate would date from approximately:

    a. 1900-1915
    b. 1800-1830
    c. 1860-1870
    d. 1840-1850

Plate J

28. T F The four-drawer chest in Plate J is an example of cottage furniture.

29. The chest was made:

    a. by a country craftsman in the early 1800's.
    b. about 1850-1860.
    c. about 1880-1890.
    d. about 1920-1930.

30. What is the primary wood in this chest?

    a. cherry
    b. pine
    c. oak
    d. poplar

Plate K

31. T F This miniature buttocks basket is worth more than a similar full-size buttocks basket.

Plate L

32. T F This is a machine-made "niddy noddy" that dates from about 1870.

Plate M

33. T F This cast-iron "snow bird" was used to hold snow on New England roofs in the late 1800's.

Plate N

Plate O

Plate P

34. T F   This is an example of a cast iron toasting fork.

35. The signature in the neck of this jar was:

    a. incised
    b. impressed
    c. neither of the above

36. The peanut butter tin dates from approximately:

    a. 1850
    b. 1860
    c. 1870
    d. after 1880

Plate Q

37. An amber fruit jar is:

   a. more difficult to find than most green jars
   b. less difficult to find than most green jars
   c. both are equally difficult to find

Plate R

38. What is this early object?

   a. a yarn winder
   b. a tape loom
   c. neither of the above

Plate S

39. How was the signature added to the piece?

   a. carved with a knife
   b. impressed with a steel plate
   c. incised with a sharp nail
   d. burned into the wood

Plate T

40. T F The maple spoon was hand-carved rather than machine-made.

Plate U

41. T F The pitcher was molded rather than hand-thrown on a potter's wheel.

Plate V

42. T F The glaze on the stoneware bowls is Albany slip.

43. T F This bowl is made of:
    a. maple
    b. walnut
    c. oak

44. What is the approximate value of this bowl?
    a. $25-$35
    b. $40-$60
    c. $65-$75
    d. more than $80

45. T F The bowl was not factory-made.

Plate W

Plate X

46. The teddy bear dates from:
    a. 1840-1860
    b. 1861-1880
    c. 1881-1895
    d. after 1900

Plate Y

47. T F The pressed paper Easter toy on the wood base is worth less than $40.

Plate Z

48. T F This tin cage was used in an early bingo parlor.

49. This was found in many homes of the late 1800's. What is it?

    a. a still bank
    b. a match safe
    c. a mouse trap
    d. none of the above

Plate Z-1

50. Which of the paint colors below would add the most value to this handled box?

    a. white
    b. blue
    c. red
    d. yellow

Plate Z-2

Scoring Key

1. c

2. b

3. b

4. d - The box was made by the Shakers.

5. a - The Shakers used copper nails because they would not rust and discolor the wood.

6. d

7. b - A problem with red ware was that foods with citric acids would interact with red ware glazes and produce a poison.

8. b

9. f - The lid used with canning jars of this form was tin held with sealing wax.

10. f - Most were made of chestnut or ash.

11. c - These were mass-produced and sold through early mail order catalogs for less than 25¢. Even though they appear to be quite early, spice boxes of this type date well after 1880.

12. c - For as late as spice boxes were made, they are dramatically over-priced today.

13. b - A butter print provided only decoration. A buttermold shaped the butter in addition to the design.

14. d - Most wood kitchen utensils were made of maple.

15. b - The crudeness of the print suggests it was obviously hand-carved.

16. b

17. b

18. c - Candlemolds have not increased in price in recent years to the degree that other early lighting pieces have.

19. c

20. a

21. d - Bucket benches are expensive. We purchas-ed this one in New York state in June, 1977, for $360.

22. b - A distinguishing feature of Nantucket baskets is the use of rattan rather than oak splint.

23. a - The Nantucket baskets were made by sailors on the island and also on the light ship off the coast.

24. c - The second distinguishing characteristic of the basket is the turned wooden bottom.

25. a

26. b

27. a

28. True - Cottage furniture was popular among the middle-class and wealthy vacationers in their eastern summer and holiday cottages in the late 1800's.

29. c

30. b - Pine was the primary wood used in cottage furniture.

31. True

32. False

33. True

34. False

35. b

36. d

37. a

38. b

39. d

40. True

41. False

42. False - Albany slip is a deep brown color.

43. a

44. d

45. True

46. d - The bears were named after Teddy Roose-
    velt who was not in office until several years
    after 1900.

47. True - The toy dates from around 1940.

48. False - This cage was designed for squirrels.

49. c

50. b

Number correct

46-50 - Apply for a position at Israel Sack, one of the
nation's great antiques showrooms.

42-46 - Apply for a position at Park Bernet, one of
the nation's great auction houses.

37-41 - Apply for a position at a local antiques shop.

32-36 - Apply for a position at a local Salvation Army
resale shop.

27-31 - Apply for a position at a local pet shop.

22-26 - Apply for help.

Suggested Reading List

A collector or would-be collector of country antiques needs a basic library prior to entering the market place. Your ability at recognizing quality reading material has already been established by your picking up this volume. Hopefully, we can increase your knowledge of country antiques and the size of your library by providing the listing of books below.

Books

1. *American Country Furniture*, Ralph and Terry Kovel - Chiltor.

2. *American Country Pottery*, Don and Carol Raycraft - Wallace-Homestead.

3. *Baskets of Rural America*, Gloria Teleki - Dutten.

4. *Colonial Lighting*, Arthur Hayward - Dover.

5. *Country Baskets*, Don and Carol Raycraft - Wallace-Homestead.

6. *Decorated Stoneware Pottery of North America*, Donald Blake Webster - Tuttle.

7. *Early Folk Pottery*, Harold Guilland - Chilton.

8. *Early American Kitchen Antiques - vol. I and II*, Don and Carol Raycraft - Wallace-Homestead.

9. *Early American Wooden Ware*, Mary Earle Gould - Tuttle.

10. *Early Lighting: A Pictorial Guide* - The Rush Light Club.

Newspapers

1. Ohio Antiques Review - Worthington, Ohio.

2. Maine Antiques Digest - Waldoboro, Maine.

3. Newtown Bee - Newtown, Connecticut.